# PSYCHOLOGICAL IMPACT OF IIRAIRA (TITLE III) ON LEGAL PERMANENT U.S. RESIDENTS AND THEIR FAMILIES

# PSYCHOLOGICAL IMPACT OF IIRAIRA (TITLE III) ON LEGAL PERMANENT U.S. RESIDENTS AND THEIR FAMILIES

✦

A Dissertation Submitted in Partial
Fulfillment of the Requirements for the
Degree of Doctor of Psychology

*Luz Maria Villanueva-Gonzalez,
M.A., Ph.D.
San Diego CA
2004*

iUniverse, Inc.
New York  Lincoln  Shanghai

# PSYCHOLOGICAL IMPACT OF IIRAIRA (TITLE III) ON LEGAL PERMANENT U.S. RESIDENTS AND THEIR FAMILIES

**A Dissertation Submitted in Partial Fulfillment of the Requirements for the Degree of Doctor of Psychology**

iUniverse books may be ordered through booksellers or by contacting:

iUniverse
2021 Pine Lake Road, Suite 100
Lincoln, NE 68512
www.iuniverse.com
1-800-Authors (1-800-288-4677)

ISBN-13: 978-0-595-37333-8 (pbk)
ISBN-13: 978-0-595-81731-3 (ebk)
ISBN-10: 0-595-37333-X (pbk)
ISBN-10: 0-595-81731-9 (ebk)

Printed in the United States of America

# Abstract of Dissertation

PSYCHOLOGICAL IMPACT OF IIRAIRA (TITLE III) ON

LEGAL PERMANENT U.S. RESIDENTS AND

THEIR FAMILIES

by

Luz Maria Villanueva-Gonzalez, M.A.

San Diego University for Integrative Studies

Historically, in relation to immigrant residents, the legal and popular attitude in the United States has been a contradictory one, alternately welcoming and rejecting. Both sought after and dismissed, non-native-born residents have lived their lives subject to ever-changing public opinion and legislative mandates. The purpose of this research is to explore the psychological effects on legal permanent U.S. residents and their families of a federal law called the Illegal Immigration Reform and Immigrant Responsibility Act of 1996 (IIRAIRA).

This descriptive study analyzed 354 self-reported, post-1996 experiences and symptomology of individuals who shared their stories on an Internet web site devoted to IIRAIRA narratives. In addition, 27 IIRAIRA-related stories from newspaper articles and 6 IIRAIRA-related stories from a community hearing were incorporated as control data.

The constant comparison method study of self-reported symptomology and experiences of legal permanent U.S. residents and their families because of IIRAIRA-related arrests, detentions, and deportations shows significant levels of PTSD and depressive symptoms resulting from family separation, economic loss, and cultural displacement. Perceived injustice and loss of confidence in the legal system because of IIRAIRA is pervasive. Two chi-square tests revealed that the number of PTSD and depressive symptoms reported are positively linked to the number of IIRAIRA-related effects reported. On average, each story reported 5.2 effects and 2.3 symptoms.

A linear correlation between all reported effects and symptoms indicated a number of notable relationships. No significant differences were found between the types of symptoms reported by detainees and those reported by their families.

The final study analysis comparing the website stories to the control data shows that symptoms are consistent in both data sets, and that while the effects distribution is not consistent between the website stories and the control data, all effects were present in both data sets.

This study demonstrates that IIRAIRA has a psychological impact on legal permanent U.S. residents and their families. The data reported by families, detainees, and third parties consistently describe similar outcomes as a result of the law. It is important that further IIRAIRA-related research be conducted; it is even more important that those who suffer from exposure to IIRAIRA should receive treatment to ameliorate its consequences. The law itself needs to be reviewed by legislators in accordance with established national and international legal norms.

The Dissertation of Luz Maria Villanueva-Gonzalez, entitled "PSYCHOLOGI-CAL IMPACT OF IIRAIRA (TITLE III) ON LEGAL PERMANENT U.S. RESIDENTS AND THEIR FAMILIES" was found to be acceptable in quality and form for publication and is therefore approved by us.

Dissertation approved by:

David Gangsei, Ph.D.

Jorge Espinoza, Ph.D.

Bill Waddell, Esq.

Joel Fick, Ph.D.

Received by:

Raymond Trybus, Ph.D., Research Director

## DEDICATION

To my children, Vanne, Christian, and Sol. You are my greatest gift of joy, and you fill my heart with endless love.

To my mother. Thank you for your prayers, and the candles you light to guide my path.

To my sisters, Isaura and Patricia. Siempre unidas.

To my friend, Noreen. ¡Sí, se puede!

# ACKNOWLEDGMENTS

I would like to thank the members of my committee for taking time from their busy schedules to provide professional guidance in their areas of expertise: Roberto Martinez, Bill Waddell, Esq., Jorge Espinoza, Ph.D., and David Gangsei, Ph.D.

I would like to thank my daughter, Vanneza, for providing a reason to finish my dissertation. I would like to thank my son Christian for being so patient when he needed my support with his schoolwork and too many times had to hear me ask him to wait. I would like to thank my son Sol for giving up a whole year of basketball, soccer, and swimming.

I would like to thank my sisters Isaura and Patricia for supporting me all through this long process.

A very special thanks goes to my friend, editor, counselor, teacher. This dissertation would not have been completed without your emotional and professional guidance, Noreen.

I would like to thank those IIRAIRA-affected families who had the courage to post their stories on the website and in other public venues. This dissertation could not have been completed without your contributions. In acknowledgment of your courage in struggling to overcome the traumas imposed by circumstances not of your choosing, I dedicate the following to you:

## Flower Boy

It's 4:30 a.m. in California. The doorbell startles mom, dad, and their oldest son awake. Men in civilian clothes, brandishing guns and handcuffs, demand to see the father, and then arrest him in front of the family. The father has no idea why, or where they are taking him, because he has done nothing wrong. The family goes into shock.

Two days later the mom finds out why the father was arrested.

The twelve-year-old son asks, "Mom, why did those men take my father away?" Mother answers, "Honey, your dad made a mistake years ago, and because of a new law written to punish legal US residents, they're going to keep him in jail. Then they'll deport him."

The boy asks, "Did my father serve his sentence?"

"Yes, he did, son, and he hasn't had any problems with the law since then."

"Mother, I don't understand. If he is legally here in this country, pays taxes, all of us are US citizens, and he already served his sentence, then why would he be taken away from us? You see, Mom, there's a boy in school named Johnny Smith. Well, his father got out of jail a year ago, and the police didn't take his father away again. There must be some mistake." Then he adds optimistically, "You know, Mom, my teacher taught me in school that you can't be punished for the same thing twice; it's in our Constitution. Don't worry; I'll talk to my teacher, and I'll see that all of this gets solved."

The next day the boy goes to his teacher. "I have a question for you. Is it true that our Constitution says that a man can never be tried twice for the same thing?"

"Of course. I'm glad you've learned this. I must be doing a good job. But why do you ask?"

"See, my father has been detained because he's a legal US resident who did something wrong years ago. And now he's being punished again; he's been put in jail and then they are going to deport him."

The boy sadly tells how he saw his father arrested while it was still dark. And then he surprises his teacher. "Why do you teach me lies—that the Constitution says that no one can ever be tried twice for the same crime? And is it somehow bad to be a legal U.S. resident?"

"Why, no," the teacher responds.

"Then why are legal residents being targeted?" The boy begins to cry. "Can you help me?"

The teacher is puzzled. "I can't help you, but if you go and speak to an immigration lawyer, he can help you." The teacher is confused and uncertain about what the boy has said. She decides to do some research, and is shocked at what she discovers: the boy is right.

The boy goes and speaks to an attorney. He explains his story, and asks for help. The attorney responds, "What I need is five thousand dollars to start…and I cannot promise you anything. All we will be doing is buying time for your father's stay of deportation, and this may mean inside the prison."

Surprised and hurt, the boy protests, "My father is the main breadwinner. We don't have that kind of extra money, and even so, why is it that you can't help my dad?"

"I am so sorry. I just can't help you. But go and speak to the judge," the attorney advises.

The boy goes to the judge and explains what happened to his father. "Judge, I know you have the power to review my father's case, and when you hear all the good things my father's done and everything he's offered this country, I know that with your power and justice you will not let us go on welfare and let them take away my father forever."

The immigration judge drops his shoulders, and in a low monotone says, "My hands are tied. I can do nothing for you, even though your father is a good man. This law took away my power. I will have to deport your father, even if he paid for his mistake, and even if it will leave you fatherless."

The boy leaves, crying and confused at what he's just heard. An old, wise man is waiting at the bus stop, holding a bundle of flowers in his arms. He sees the boy crying disconsolately.

"Hello. May I ask why you are crying, my child?"

"Well, see, in my school I have learned false information. My country does not have equal laws for everyone and the judges have no power. And my father will be taken away from me."

The boy explains how the 1996 Illegal Immigration Reform And Immigrant Responsibility Act (IIRAIRA) will leave him unprotected without his father, and how his faith in his school and in his government has been shaken.

The wise man reassures him. "Don't worry. Go and take this flower to the lawmakers as a reminder that today, you and your family are alive like this blossom. Tell them that as every day goes by, this flower will die, and so will people's hearts and spirits. Tell them that they are the ones that are responsible to you and to many others for allowing such an injustice to be committed. Tell them that they must answer to you, to me, and to the whole world for letting such a thing happen in this great country of ours—the United States of America."

From
U.S. Children and Families Affected by IIRAIRA
American Friends Service Committee
San Diego, CA (619) 233-4114

# Contents

# List of Figures

# List of Tables

# 1

# *Introduction*

An unjust law in itself is an act of violence.

—Gandhi

Historically, in relation to immigrant residents, the legal and popular attitude in the United States has been a contradictory one, alternately welcoming and rejecting. Both sought after and dismissed, non-native-born residents have lived their lives subject to ever-changing public opinion and legislative mandates. Sometimes they are actively recruited, as were the Chinese immigrants who helped build the railroads. Other times they are driven from the country because of the larger community's racial, political, social, and economic fears.

As a reaction to the 1995 Oklahoma City bombing, in response to perceived foreign terrorism, Congress sought to deport domestic "criminal aliens" by enacting the Antiterrorism and Effective Death Penalty Act of 1996 (ADEPA) and the Illegal Immigration Reform and Immigrant Responsibility Act of 1996 (IIRAIRA). Retroactively reclassifying scores of rehabilitated legal permanent U.S. residents with criminal records as aggravated felons, making them automatically subject to deportation, IIRAIRA provided justification for the massive roundups, detentions, and deportations of immigrants that began immediately after its passage and continue to the present.

As originally enacted, IIRAIRA included no allowances for extenuating legal circumstances. Thus, no one affected by the law could introduce such conditions as expungements, misdemeanor classification, successful completion of sentence, length of time since commission of offense, subsequent rehabilitation, military status, marriage to a U.S. citizen, or current community standing. Overriding the legal point that not all offenses are punishable by deportation, and denying the legal right of access to judicial review, IIRAIRA mandated that the main criteria for deportable status was whether a resident's criminal record contained one or

1

more of a large number of offenses retroactively reclassified as aggravated felonies. The effects on the immigrant community nationwide were immediate.

The version of IIRAIRA referred to in this study is the one initially written into law, since that version affected the first large-scale number of legal permanent residents. To date, the only significant change to the law occurred on July 20, 2000, when the Supreme Court ruled that any residents legally in the United States for at least seven years, who had committed a crime before April 1996, to which they had pled guilty, would be eligible to apply for a 212c waiver to fight their deportation in court, where they would have an opportunity to prove that they were rehabilitated and had family ties.

This change affected only a small number of the country's legal resident population who had completed their served time before 1996. The legal status of those thousands who were seized, detained, and deported after1996 is still determined by the provisions of IIRAIRA as they were originally written.

IIRAIRA, created in the context of a decades-long political atmosphere increasingly harsh towards immigrants, is an example of ever more regressive federal and state legislation. Creators and supporters in Congress saw it as a solution to what has often been labeled "the immigration problem." Lamar Smith (R-TX), who helped draft and enact IIRAIRA, stated, "The children are the innocent parties. The real answer is to deport their parents" (Colon, 1999, p. B1).

Waddell (1999) explained that by expanding the definition of aggravated felony and applying it retroactively, IIRAIRA guaranteed that the public would assume all legal permanent residents are dangerous individuals who could justifiably be rounded up by armed officials. With no prior notice, people could be seized at home, at work, returning from a vacation trip, standing in line at the citizenship office, during the day or in the middle of the night, in the presence of spouse and children. "The aggravated felon is a creature of Congressional making and in 1996 Congress created literally thousands of them overnight" (Waddell, 1999, p. 191).

The use of legislative language to influence perception has a powerful effect. Permanent legal U.S. residents labeled and perceived as criminals can justifiably be distrusted, deprived of their rights and their livelihood, separated from family and friends, jailed, and deported. IIRAIRA's language allows community members to excuse what is happening to their neighbors and co-workers as something necessary for the good of the country. Such conditions may be breeding grounds for mental illness, and those affected can rightly be classified as victims.

Rationalizations for such extreme national measures and community acceptance of them make legal residents' voices unlikely to be heard when they question how someone who has paid for a past crime can be punished a second time, even more harshly, for the same offense.

What are the thoughts of this muted population? How do they feel? What losses are they experiencing? What is the law's effect on their psyche, individually and collectively? Seeking to answer some of these questions, this research analyzes self-reports in order to explore the psychological impact of IIRAIRA on legal permanent U.S. residents and their families.

## STATEMENT OF THE PROBLEM

According to Espenshade, Baraka, and Huber (1997), the purpose of the Illegal Immigration Reform and Immigrant Responsibility Act of 1996 (IIRAIRA) is to combat illegal immigration, ensure that those who sponsor legal immigrants are financially self-sufficient, and deport criminal legal residents. This research study will focus on one aspect of the law: the deportation of legal permanent U.S. residents who have an already satisfied criminal conviction. The deportation mandate is contained in TITLE III of the law. Within this dissertation, it is understood that unless otherwise indicated, all references are to IIRAIRA (TITLE III).

The original law specified that legal permanent U.S. residents who served a sentence in the past can be retroactively reclassified as aggravated felons, re-apprehended, confined indefinitely, and removed from the country, with no judicial review. A legal permanent U.S. resident is one who fulfills all criteria for living in the country as if he/she were native-born, and who, unless his/her status changes, is entitled to nearly all the privileges of citizenship except the right to vote (Bender, 1996). To the resident, such a designation connotes security, stability, the kind of reliability that flows from legality, the assumption that one is not a visitor but a permanent member of a society that has publicly acknowledged that relationship.

However, a number of U.S. court decisions have put forth a different view. The recurrence of a "guest" metaphor to justify deportations shows that courts have been influenced by theories of common law property: residency can be revoked at will, as if it were no more than a verbal agreement between two individuals, with no binding legal force. Kanstroom (2000) believes that such manipulation of residency regulations and residents' lives occurs because courts sometimes view deportation laws as tools for social control, not necessarily limited to the border or to the legal admission process. He says they follow what might best be termed an "eternal probation" or an "eternal guest" model, ignoring the idea of "permanence" integral to the category of "permanent legal resident." The strongest version of such a model would suggest that non-native-born residents, including legal permanent residents, are allowed to remain in the country only at the whim of the government. Therefore, they may be deported at the whim of the government (Kanstroom, 2000, p. 1907).

Actions stemming from "the lawful permanent resident as guest" model are further justified when courts minimize the legal, social, psychological, and personal costs of deportation. Ignoring deportees' experience that deportation may "deprive a man of all that makes life worth living" and may be, "at times, the equivalent of banishment or exile," the Supreme Court has repeatedly asserted, as case records indicate, that deportation is, in general, neither a criminal process nor a punishment. A court that makes decisions based on such a model feels justified in deporting residents simply because they are perceived to be threats, criminals. No real proof of threat or criminality is required. Such exclusionary acts are completely arbitrary, and any situation can be interpreted to justify any exclusion (Kanstroom, 2000, p. 1914).

Judicial review is a cornerstone of the U.S. legal system. When a broadly written law of major significance subverts judicial review, confusion and tragedy inevitably follow. IIRAIRA mandated that in addition to being reclassified as aggravated felons and being denied protection from double jeopardy, permanent legal residents were to be banned from the U.S. for life. The law prohibited judges from examining any case to decide whether compelling circumstances warranted a change in status. IIRAIRA aims to "[curtail] the never-ending legal appeals process that was used by immigration lawyers to keep their clients in the United States until they found a sympathetic judge who would grant suspension of deportation" (Jordan, 1995, p. 1).

IIRAIRA's stated intention is to remove dangerous criminals from the United States. The 1996 law replaces the longstanding federal policy that already deports any legal permanent resident who has served a prison sentence of five years or more. The evidence regarding IIRAIRA, however, suggests that it is being used to arrest, imprison, and deport an astonishing number whose crimes were petty, committed long ago, already paid for through time served, or deemed insufficient for prosecution. Since 1996, thousands of legal permanent U.S. residents have been deported. In 1998 alone, "56,011 were removed for criminal convictions" (Waddell, 1999, p. 194).

IIRAIRA has condemned some to imprisonment for life. A legal permanent U.S. resident whose country of origin does not have a diplomatic relationship with the U.S. (Cuba, Iran, Iraq, North Korea, Libya, Vietnam, Laos, and the People's Republic of China) cannot be returned to his/her country of origin and must, therefore, under IIRAIRA, be detained indefinitely in the United States. Waddell (1999) reports that "in October of 1998, the INS indicated that its detention facilities held 2,500 'lifers'" (p. 194). A subsequent Supreme Court decision amended the status of lifers by ruling that they could be detained no longer than 6 months; however, they remain in deportation proceedings indefinitely and are subject to strict administrative conditions imposed by the INS (Zadvydas v. Davis, 2001). Overall, detention remains mandatory for all legal permanent residents apprehended by the INS, and in most cases is in effect as long as deportation proceedings are ongoing.

Punitive laws have devastating human consequences. Because of IIRAIRA, detainees and their family members can undergo dramatic negative life changes, including humiliation, economic loss, cultural displacement, and social relocation. It would be surprising if the victims of this law did not experience symptoms of such psychological conditions as anxiety, depression, and post-traumatic stress disorder.

IIRAIRA made the legal resident community vulnerable to the psychological trauma of an overnight change in status. People went to bed one night as legal permanent U.S. residents, equal to citizens in every major category except voting. They awoke the next morning as unwelcome guests/felons, with the loss of rights that such a status change implies. Lifelong legal residents who adopted U.S. culture and values, paid taxes, raised their own families here, and considered this country their home were placed in a position of maximum uncertainty and fear.

One of the major provisions of IIRAIRA, retroactivity, has been fought in court as a violation of the constitutional tenet that a person cannot be tried twice for the same crime (Prakash, 1997). Under IIRAIRA, someone who earlier satisfied the judicial system for what was at that time a non-deportable crime can be subsequently re-arrested, re-charged, and permanently deported because the paid-for crime has been retroactively reclassified as a more serious offense. This may lead to an additional lifelong punishment of separation from family, as well as deep psychological wounds.

The passage of IIRAIRA is of great concern for sociological and psychological reasons. There is abundant anecdotal evidence that the law's provisions and the manner in which they are executed are destroying reputations and lives, creating the potential for lifelong adverse psychological effects. Legal permanent U.S. resident families report experiencing increased fear and feelings of vulnerability because of the law. Children affected by IIRAIRA are at risk for adopting a negative self-image, suffering from emotional distress, and developing anger towards government/authority. The larger society has received the message that legal permanent U.S. residents are expendable, second-class citizens with fewer rights, and that they may be mocked as humans. A recent example of the latter is the 1997 Chandler raids in Arizona, five days during which over 400 people were rounded up by police and the border patrol, based solely on suspicion of undocumented status. The predictable outcome was that U.S. citizens and legal permanent U.S. residents suffered the same fate as the undocumented workers: detention and deportation to Mexico (Flores & Duran, 1998).

Under IIRAIRA, the circumstances surrounding domestic violence have become more problematic for permanent legal U.S. resident families. The law requires that a man charged with physically abusing his wife attend therapy and possibly serve jail time. Serving time and attending therapy have been proven to help many families. Regarding batterer intervention programs, the Office of Justice Programs (2003) reports that men who attend treatment for longer periods of time, such as 26 weeks, have a better prognosis relative to committing less violent crimes; another positive variable for lower re-incidence is if the batterer is employed, married, and/or owns his home. However, in the permanent legal U.S. resident community, where because of IIRAIRA domestic violence has now become cause for deportation, women may be less likely to call the police for assistance and the family may not get the help it needs. In this way, IIRAIRA creates more danger for these families, particularly for wives and children.

Similarly, when the retroactive crime of either parent is child abuse (physical, sexual, neglect), IIRAIRA precludes the rehabilitated permanent legal U.S. resident parent from being treated as any parent would be in a similar situation. Under IIRAIRA, even if the abuse occurred decades ago and the family is currently re-integrated, the mitigating issue of the parent's rehabilitation is not taken into consideration. Deporting one such parent instantly creates an unprepared single-parent household with the potential for a number of negative possibilities: the cost of caring for the children may have to be shared by the government; the change in economic status is likely to engender debilitating emotions such as anger, depression, despair; the children may develop behavior problems because of the traumatic loss of family stability; the remaining parent is likely to feel the psychological effects of being deserted, desperate, lonely, and overwhelmed.

IIRAIRA has created an ethical dilemma for healthcare professionals—doctors, social workers, counselors, psychologists, psychiatrists—regarding reporting any domestic problems in permanent legal U.S. resident households. When caregivers who are familiar with IIRAIRA become aware of family problems that should be reported to authorities, they are faced with the terrible knowledge that not reporting a situation will allow it to continue, while reporting it will bring the families to the attention of those who will deport them. And those professionals who are not yet aware of the law's consequences can inadvertently create the same risk for their clients by handling situations as they did pre-IIRAIRA.

In addition to being faced with federal-level repercussions created by IIRAIRA, members of the legal profession can find themselves in a similar bind at the state level. Prosecutors, defense attorneys, judges, and probation officers must try to negotiate an appropriate sentence that will not at the same time subject a defendant to deportation when it would be a punishment out of proportion to the crime (Ippolito & Badie, 2001).

In regard to IIRAIRA, just as in any situation, the level of understanding varies within the community. While many rehabilitated legal U.S. permanent residents apprehended under the law are encouraged by those closest to them, some can experience loss of support from family and friends who mistakenly conclude that past guilt automatically guarantees present guilt. Such IIRAIRA-affected residents cannot move on from their past because the law brings it to life again, opening the door to possible judgments from family, friends, and community, and imposing the burden of renewed shame. All legal permanent U.S. residents who in the past committed a crime and who become aware of IIRAIRA are at risk for a life of apprehension, fearing the moment the INS will take them to jail and likely deport them.

The effects of IIRAIRA are felt worldwide, in every country to which legal permanent U.S. residents are deported. According to the San (2003), many IIRAIRA deportees from the United States are deported to Tijuana, Baja California, Mexico, a country to which they may have few, if any, connections. They find themselves suffering emotionally because they have lost the vital support of U.S. family ties and do not know where to go. This is of great concern to city officials because a large number of deported individuals become part of Tijuana's "floating population," an amorphous mix of homeless/jobless men, women, and children. According to San, those who cannot find a job or any type of stable support are more likely to form alliances with people in the streets, where the availability of drugs may offer what looks like a way to deal with their situation.

Some deportees who become desperate when they find themselves jobless, unconnected to their country of origin, and separated from their families, take the enormous chance of re-entering the U.S. illegally. According to Waddell (1999), "Those caught attempting to enter the U.S., or found here after removal, subject themselves to up to 20 years in federal prison" (p. 194). This can impose not only a huge cost on taxpayers but a lifelong emotional impact on the affected families.

# STUDY OBJECTIVE

Given that the widespread domestic and international effects of IIRAIRA are ongoing, it seems logical to assume it would be a subject of interest to researchers. But while it is true that journalists and legal scholars have looked into the law and its ramifications, social scientists have not yet made inroads into studying the subject. To date, there are no scientific data on the psychological condition of deportees, their families, or the community of permanent legal U.S. residents affected by IIRAIRA. This study will try to gauge some of the effects of the drastic changes caused by the law.

The goal of the study is to understand and analyze how IIRAIRA is affecting deportees and their families. The researcher will explore the nature of social and psychological damages suffered, and collect data related to the experiences and symptoms of affected families and individuals.

Both the deportee and family members may experience depression, anxiety, and post-traumatic stress disorder. The uncertainty of the deportee's life and the struggles of those left behind who are trying to stay rooted in the U.S. can exacerbate the effects of negative life stressors, causing them to be experienced for longer periods of time and to a greater degree.

# DEFINITIONS

Definitions, as offered, are solely for the purposes of this study.

**Aggravated felon:** A legal permanent U.S. resident who was reclassified under IIRAIRA and put in deportation proceedings.

**Alien:** "[A]ny person not a citizen or national of the United States" (Bender, 1996, p. 11).

**Anxiety:** "Type of abnormal behavior characterized by unrealistic, irrational fear" (Huffman, Vernoy, & Vernoy, 1997, p. 485).

**Custody:** The condition of a legal permanent U.S. resident with a reclassified deportable conviction under IIRAIRA, who is detained by the INS while awaiting removal to his/her country of origin.

**Deportee:** A legal permanent U.S. resident with a reclassified deportable conviction under IIRAIRA, who has been deported from the U.S.

**Depression:** "A long-lasting depressed mood that interferes with the ability to function, feel pleasure, or maintain interest in life" (Huffman et al., 1997, p. 498).

**Detainee:** A legal permanent U.S. resident with a reclassified deportable conviction under IIRAIRA, who is in INS custody while awaiting deportation.

**Double jeopardy:** "The Fifth Amendment says that no person shall be 'twice put in jeopardy of life and limb.' This means that once a defendant has been acquitted of a crime, he or she is protected from being tried again for the same crime" (Miller, 1999, p. 160).

**Family member:** A spouse, child, or blood relative who is directly affected by the potential or actual deportation of a legal permanent U.S. resident.

**Immigrant:** "[E]very alien except an alien who is within one of the classes of nonimmigrant aliens" (Bender, 1996, p. 13).

**Immigration and Naturalization Service (INS):** Federal agency within the U.S. Department of Justice (DOJ) that administers the nation's immigrations laws. "Includes material on INS forms and fees, immigration services and benefits, law enforcement and border management, field offices, laws, regulations, and guides" (retrieved October 2003 from http://www.britannica.com). Following a 2003 reorganization, the agency was divided into two branches: the Bureau of Immigration Customs Enforcement and the Bureau of Immigration Services. This study uses the title INS, since the agency had that title at the time IIRAIRA was enacted.

**Judicial review:** The power of the court to determine the constitutionality of the actions of the executive, legislative, and judicial branches of government, and to decide whether a law or other governmental action violates the Constitution (Miller, 1999).

**Legal permanent U.S. resident:** "A person having been lawfully accorded the privilege of residing permanently in the United States as an immigrant, in accordance with the immigration laws, such status not having changed" (Bender, 1996, p. 22).

**Lifer:** Legal permanent U.S. resident with a reclassified conviction under IIRAIRA, who is in deportation status and whose country of origin is not willing to receive him/her. Under IIRAIRA, in such a situation, the U.S. attorney general may retain the individual in custody for life.

**Order of deportation:** The order of a special inquiry officer or other such administrative officer to whom the attorney general has delegated the responsibility for determining whether an alien is deportable, concluding that the alien is deportable or ordering deportation. (Bender, 1996).

**Post-traumatic stress disorder (PTSD):** Type of anxiety disorder that follows an overwhelming, traumatic event (Huffman, et al., 1997).

**Retroactivity:** Extending, in scope or effect, to a prior time or to conditions that existed or originated in the past, especially: made effective as of a date prior to enactment, promulgation, or imposition (retrieved October 2003 from http://www.mw.com).

# 2

# *Literature Review*

## HISTORY OF LEGISLATED EXCLUSIONS

Martinez (n.d.) writes that in order to understand how IIRAIRA impacts the permanent legal U.S. resident community, we must look at some recent historical events informing the country's current political reality.

On June 2, 1919, bombs exploded in eight American cities. Then-Attorney General A. Mitchell Palmer, suspecting the involvement of Russian and Eastern European residents, who were known as "alien reds," ordered a massive roundup, detention, and deportation of immigrants. Under provisions of the Espionage Act of 1917, the Sedition Act of 1918, and the Deportation Act of 1918, thousands were held in secret, without bail, denied access to lawyers, and hastily deported. Willette (2003) says that the government arrested, detained, and deported at least 10,000, without revealing their names and without charging them with any crime.

In hindsight, Palmer's actions are seen as vindictive. "Historians generally contend that the raids were unwarranted, anti-immigrant, and fueled by the political motivation of Attorney General Palmer and by public hysteria stemming from Palmer's edicts. The raids are characterized as an illegal usurpation of government authority" (Willette, 2003, p. 13).

In the book *Decade of Betrayal*, Balderrama and Rodriguez (2002) focus on the 1930s, the Great Depression years, when the federal government repeated the Palmer-like raids—though this time citing economics—and ordered roundups and deportations of tens of thousands of Chicanos/Mexicans from California and other parts of the Southwest. Federal agents and local authorities apprehended people at dance halls, markets, and theaters where Chicanos/Mexicans were known to gather.

According to Magagnini (2003), about one million people of Mexican descent were deported during the 1930s, including thousands of American-born children who had never been to Mexico. The official justification was that 25 million "real Americans" were unemployed because immigrants were taking away jobs.

Jones (2003) relates that on behalf of the many deportees who lost homes during the 1930s, federal-level class action suits are now being contemplated by the City of Los Angeles, the State of California, and individual defendants, alleging violations of constitutional rights.

In July of 2003, at a gathering in Los Angeles, California, State Senator Joe Dunn (D-Santa Ana), referring to the 1930s deportations, vowed to "bring the ugly episode to light—and possibly seek reparations similar to those paid to Japanese-Americans interned during World War II—so that history doesn't repeat itself" (Magagnini, 2003).

A number of the hearing attendees, elderly men and women who were children during the Great Depression, still remember the last time they saw their fathers. Though encouraged by the discussion of reparations for the deportation damages, some are emotionally conflicted about it. Raymond Rodriguez, co-author of *Decade of Betrayal*, says "My dad left in 1936, when I was 10…I never saw [him] again. How is anybody going to compensate me for my loss?" (Magagnini, 2003, p. 1A).

Another hearing attendee, Emilia Castaneda, recalls the agony of having been deported to Mexico during the 1930s, a nine-year-old with a Shirley Temple doll, living among people who made it obvious that she and her family were not welcome. When she finally learned enough Spanish to go to school, she was called a *repatriada* (repatriate), which deeply offended her because she knew she was an American.

Recounting her story as an adult, Castaneda said that both men and women deportees were objects of criticism. Women were censured for their cooking, their dress, and the way they spoke to men. Their husbands were judged not "man enough" to stay up north and defend their right to be in the U.S.

The pattern of deportations continued during the 1940s. In response to the Japanese attack on Pearl Harbor the morning of December 7, 1941, President Franklin Roosevelt authorized the military to detain Japanese-American citizens, legal residents, and immigrants. Thousands were removed from their homes and placed in camps for the duration of World War II. Thousands more were deported; in one citation, Willette (2003) mentions 4,724. Using the justification of national security, the government carried out the detentions and deportations under the Immigration and Nationality Act of 1940 and the Alien Registration Act of 1940 (Willette, 2003).

It is estimated that in the 1950s, during the INS-organized action known as "Operation Wetback," over one million men, women, and children were deported from the U.S., either because they actually were Chicano/Mexican or because they simply looked as if they were (Martinez, n.d.).

Assessing the legislated deportations in 1919 during the Palmer raids, in the 1930s during the depression, and in the 1950s during Operation Wetback, Willette (2003) demonstrates the existence of a predictable pattern: when crises erupt in the United States, immigrants, legal residents, and citizens are rounded up, detained, and deported by the government, under policies that are routinely, often hastily, written to justify the execution of detention and deportation legislation. To cite one example, in the space of just 23 years, Congress enacted the Espionage Act of 1917, the Sedition Act of 1918, the Deportation Act of 1918, the Immigration and Nationality Act of 1940, and the Alien Registration Act of 1940.

Today, the IIRAIRA law has continued the American tradition of legislated exclusions.

## SUMMARY OF IIRAIRA

In April of 1995, reacting to the Oklahoma City bombing that was initially mis-labeled as a foreign terrorist attack, Congress followed historical patterns and passed deportation legislation, this time in acts known as Antiterrorism and Effective Death Penalty Act (ADEPA) and IIRAIRA (Mace & Roane, 2001).

On September 30, 1996, the Illegal Immigration Reform and Immigrant Responsibility Act (IIRAIRA) of 1996 went into effect. Prior to the law's passage, the business community mounted an intense lobbying effort to have Congress include amnesty and legalization provisions for certain groups of immigrant workers. Not only were these provisions rejected, but the final version of IIRAIRA incorporates some of the most draconian measures ever taken against legal permanent U.S. residents and illegal immigrants (Fragomen, 1997). Fragomen offers a concise summary of IIRAIRA:

> Title I deals with border enforcement, requiring that the number of border patrol agents be doubled to 10,000 over five years, and that a fourteen-mile-long fence be built along the Mexican border.
>
> Title II covers enhanced enforcement and penalties against alien smuggling and document fraud.
>
> Title III completely revamps existing deportation and exclusion proceed-

ings, allows for summary exclusion, and provides new grounds for exclusion and deportation.

Title IV, which covers employer sanctions, calls for a reduction in the number of documents that are acceptable for I-9 purposes and provides for three pilot programs to test electronic verification of an employee's work status.

Title V contains the welfare provisions, which have undergone significant revisions.

Title VI includes stringent changes to existing refugee and asylum procedures, as well as numerous miscellaneous provisions, including the extension of the "Conrad State 20" Program (which permits waivers of the two-year foreign residence requirement for foreign medical graduates) and the Visa Waiver Pilot Program. (p. 438)

## IIRAIRA's Unique Provision

TITLE III, the provision of IIRAIRA whose effects are the focus of this study, allows the Immigration and Naturalization Service to detain and deport legal permanent U.S. residents, previously convicted of felonies, whose cases have already been fully resolved by the system in one way or another. The law justifies this extreme measure by arbitrarily retroactively redefining as aggravated felonies—and therefore deportable crimes—many simple felonies and minor offenses.

IIRAIRA overthrows the existing system for deportations, generating massive roundups of residents in their homes, in the workplace, going on or coming from trips. When stopped by the police for any reason, when already serving an unrelated sentence, when at the INS offices to attend citizenship meetings or to renew their status as required by law, residents are seized and put in detention.

IIRAIRA was enacted in part because members of Congress perceived immigrants as a threat to the U.S. lifestyle (McBride, 1999). Kanstroom (2000) mentions several reasons given to justify deportation, such as that the country needs to rid itself of those who possess undesirable qualities, while at the same time controlling the growth of serious crime. Moreover, as a nation we need to "maintain the credibility and legitimacy of our immigration laws" (p. 1890).

The facts, however, do not always correspond to the perceptions. Butcher and Piehl (1999) compared records of criminal aliens incarcerated in California prisons during the years 1986, 1990, and 1996 with those of native-born inmates during the same years. They found that the crime rate for aliens was lower than that for citizens, despite the fact that most of the aliens had a lower level of education. These findings do not support the rationale offered for the passage of IIRAIRA: that such a law is necessary because aliens are disproportionately responsible for the country's crime rate.

# RESPONSE TO IIRAIRA

Assessments of IIRAIRA have been scathing. The *Harvard Law Review* has sharply criticized the law because of its consequences, noting that it has "had a wide range of negative implications for noncitizens in many areas of law, including the law of retroactivity, the right to appointed counsel, the Fourth Amendment exclusionary rule, the privilege against self-incrimination, and the right against cruel and unusual punishment" (Kanstroom, 2000, p. 1896).

The law has been denounced because it has "caused immense hardship and suffering to thousands of people and has sought to eliminate the judicial branch entirely from any meaningful role in decisions of the most fundamental kind" (Kanstroom, 2000, p. 1935).

In a recent decision, the Ninth Circuit Court of Appeals also took the authors of IIRAIRA to task. "The purpose of the statute according to the government is unlike any other the court has approved of in upholding retroactive legislation" (U.S. Ninth Circuit, 2003, p. 15143). The court found that IIRAIRA violated three of the rules for retroactive legislation. Such legislation must be limited temporally; that is, not reach too far into the past. Retroactive laws can "operate retroactively to spread the costs of a current social problem," but they must be subject to an "independent rationale" from Congress regarding why they were necessary. According to the Ninth Circuit, IIRAIRA fails these tests. In unusually strong language, the court itself describes the injustice underpinning IIRAIRA:

> Does the government consider all such immigrants dangerous to society? Such a belief is plainly irrational because it sweeps in a broad class of immigrants who have committed a crime at some time in the remote past, no matter how young they were when they committed the offence, no matter how they have straightened out their lives, no matter whether they have become loyal hardworking employees, good neighbors, taxpayers and an asset to their communities, and no matter whether they have married, cared for their American-born children, etc. It is arbitrary to assume that all such persons

threaten our society because they committed a crime at some time in the past. (U.S. Ninth Circuit, 2003, p. 15145)

# IIRAIRA-RELATED ARRESTS, DETENTIONS, AND DEPORTATIONS

In regard to legal permanent U.S. residents, the total number of IIRAIRA-related detentions and deportations is difficult to determine, since statistics often combine categories, such as undocumented and documented. Detention/deportation estimates are in the hundreds of thousands. In 1998, 56,011 were deported (Waddell, 1999). Deportations for 2001 were 71,994 and for 2002 were 70,759 (U.S. Citizenship and Immigration Services, 2002). Though striking, the numbers are deceptive because they do not indicate that deportation traumatizes not only the deportee but also the immediate and the extended family. The examples below are anecdotal in nature, but they chronicle some of the substantial psychological and social ramifications of deportation:

- Two weeks after a father, a legal permanent U.S. resident, was deported to Colombia because in 1989 he had been convicted for selling a $10 bag of marijuana, his 17-year-old son committed suicide (McDonnell, 1998b).

- A 47-year-old single father of four was detained under IIRAIRA because in 1993 he had sold some marijuana. He had had no re-incidence, nor had he violated his probation. He is now serving a sentence a second time. One of his daughters explained to a journalist "My dad paid for his crime. They're now punishing us." She has now become a mother, father, cook and nurse to her younger siblings. After revealing that she does not know how the children will survive if their father is deported, she said, "My father is a good person. They're taking our father from us, and we're not able to live a normal life" (Maxwell, 1998, p. 1D).

It is not difficult to find journalistic reports of the injustices resulting from IIRAIRA. Most major newspapers in the United States have carried one or more stories describing the effects of the law. The majority focus on the pain and suffering inflicted on those who do not appear to "deserve" such treatment; very few comment on truly dangerous felons who have been detained and deported.

IIRAIRA-related newspaper accounts typically provide a brief case summary. Speaking through a reporter for the *Miami Herald*, the president of the American Bar Association, Philip S. Anderson, describes the case of Olufolake Olaleye:

> The Immigration and Naturalization Service has ordered the Atlanta mother of two deported because she was convicted six years ago of shoplifting baby outfits worth $14.99. Olaleye, a Nigerian who became a permanent resident in 1990, has two small children, both born in the United States. She has supported herself and her family as a gas-station cashier and never has received public benefits since she legally entered the United States in 1984. (Anderson, 1999, p. 19A)

Typically, accounts also describe the economic, social, and emotional effects of IIRAIRA:

> …Last June she was ordered deported. She is appealing…. Is the hard-working mother of two, with no other offense, a threat to our society? Did Congress really intend this law be used to separate a mother from her children, or to uproot her children from their country of citizenship? (Anderson, 1999, p. 19A)

As seen in the quote above, writers of IIRAIRA-related stories inject analysis into their textual descriptions. Expressions of dismay over injustice are frequent. The following pattern is repeated in most IIRAIRA-related newspaper accounts:

- Textual description of the facts that establish a relationship with IIRAIRA
- Textual description of the effects that detention and deportation have on individuals and family members
- Expressions of injustice by the author of the article

# INDIVIDUAL REPORTS OF
# IIRAIRA-RELATED EFFECTS

Those directly impacted by IIRAIRA provide another primary source for documentation of its effects. The law's passage coincided with the rise of the Internet as a tool for communicating and organizing information. Several websites are devoted to fighting the injustices associated with IIRAIRA. At least one allows individuals to publish their own stories, describing ways in which the 1996 law has affected their lives.

At the time this information was downloaded from the Internet (August 8, 2003), 354 individuals had posted their stories on the IIRAIRA-related website "Stories from the Town Meeting" (http://www.ilw.com/micasa/tm.htm). These narratives often follow a similar pattern, describing facts of the case, effects on the detainee, and examples of injustices. Many of the cases deal explicitly with TITLE III of IIRAIRA. At the same time, a number are unrelated; they describe negative effects relating to other areas of immigration law. Some website entries are not accounts, but simply expressions of anger, sympathy, or solidarity in fighting the perceived injustices.

# PERCEIVED INJUSTICE AS AN INTENSIFIER OF
# PSYCHOLOGICAL AND SOCIAL TRAUMA

It is clear that injustice and psychological/social damage are related, as it is clear that any extraordinarily negative life events have consequences for the well-being of those affected. Suffering and injustice cause pain and social disruption that have psychological consequences. Conditions such as anxiety, depression, and post-traumatic stress disorder are strongly connected to an individual's reaction to adverse life events. Sudden violence, the unexpected loss of a loved one, rape, and involuntary displacement from one's home are often triggering events for severe psychological trauma. The individuals and families affected by IIRAIRA-related detention and deportation frequently report suffering caused by a family member being seized while at home, by the sudden loss of a loved one, and by an event of unforeseen violence in a world revealed as unjust.

# RELATIONSHIP BETWEEN PERCEPTION OF INJUSTICE AND SYMPTOMS

Research with felons and malpractice litigants shows that perception of fairness depends on the level of involvement in a process and the degree to which one is respected and trusted. If one is free to present personal views and evidence, and has a real opportunity to influence decisions, the process is seen to be fair. It is when an individual has no voice that a sense of injustice is aroused (Sydeman, 1997).

By creating what was perceived to be an unjust situation, researchers in controlled experiments have provoked emotional states of anger and frustration. These emotions were highest when an unfair procedure caused an unfavorable outcome (Krehbeil & Cropanzano, 2000).

When individuals endure the Holocaust, when children suffer the horrors of war, when penned-up families live under guard, when loved ones are arbitrarily seized and taken away, victims' voices are stifled by a procedure that is inherently unfair. Natural responses of anger and frustration devolve into a sense of helplessness and despair that is accompanied by a heightened fear of potential threat.

Though strong, the link between real/perceived injustices and intensified negative effects is not always explicit. Indeed, those who survive and "move on" may be surprisingly resilient and successful in pursuing their life goals while still experiencing the negative effects in their daily lives (Sagi-Schwartz, 2003; Yaari, 1999).

If IIRAIRA is perceived as unjust, as legal scholars and victims claim, then it is highly likely that attendant social and psychological effects will be intensified by this perception.

# DISCRIMINATION, PERCEPTION OF INJUSTICE, AND SYMPTOMS

The discrimination encountered daily by minorities in America offers another example of how perceived injustice can affect psychological and physical health. It is reported in *Mental Health: Surgeon General* (1999) that for some African-Americans, perceived discrimination is associated with psychological distress, a lower sense of well-being, self-reported ill health, and the number of days confined to bed (Ren, Amick, & Williams, 1999; Williams, Yu, Jackson, & Anderson, 1997). The same study examined the psychological distress and depression caused by large-scale discrimination and the generalized distress and depression caused by day-to-day perceived discrimination, in order to gauge the association between these two forms of discrimination and poor mental health. When the results were compared with those related to other commonly studied stressful life events such as job loss, divorce, or the death of a loved one, the consequences were similar in magnitude (Kessler, Mickelson, & Williams, 1999).

According to *Mental Health: Surgeon General* (1999), perceived discrimination (which can be understood as a subset of injustice) can lead to symptoms of depression and anxiety. When injustice is piled on top of trauma, there is an amplifying effect on all concerned. Clearly, as this study shows, not only does the individual IIRAIRA-affected deportee suffer, the family suffers as well. The trauma experienced by those most affected may justify clinical diagnosis of post-traumatic stress disorder (PTSD).

## EFFECTS OF TRAUMA ON SURVIVORS

A review of the literature shows this sense of injustice aggravates the intensity of any trauma's negative effects. As a consequence, dysthymic symptomology may persist for a lifetime. Holocaust survivors who endured grave injustice many years ago still report more pain and higher rates of depression than do others who escaped those World War II atrocities (Yaari, 1999). Researchers who focused on psychological symptomology among Holocaust survivors found that they displayed more anxiety, post-traumatic stress, and unresolved trauma than comparison subjects. Holocaust survivors were not, however, impaired in general adaptation (Sagi-Schwartz, 2003).

Similarly, children in war zones suffer long-term reactions to incomprehensible traumas. Thabat (2002) studied Palestinian children exposed to traumas such as loss of housing and violent attacks, and compared them to young Iraqi Kurds, displaced Iranian children, and displaced Croatian children. The author found severe and pervasive post-traumatic stress reactions: "More than twice as many children exposed to bombardment and home demolition reported severe to very severe post-traumatic stress reactions than those who were not exposed" (Thabat, 2002, p. 1803).

Children also suffer major psychological and social consequences when their families undergo an overnight change in structure from two-parent to single-parent, with its attendant economic upheaval, or when they are forced to involuntarily relocate to a new cultural/social environment. The loss of a parent, whether as the result of death, divorce, or separation for any reason, temporary or permanent, has similar consequences for a child (http://www.hec.ohio-state. edu/famlife/divorce/effects.htm).

# EFFECTS OF TRAUMA ON FAMILIES

Under the best of conditions, single parenting is a challenge. The difficulty of that task is increased when families are forced to cope with negative events and circumstances not of their own making. Research has shown that during such periods of turmoil, both adults and children undergo major psychological and social changes. Rumberger and Larson (1998) indicate that school dropout rates, relocation, and single-parent households are related. Scanlon and Devine (2001) have shown that poverty, life-cycle changes, and single-parent households are risk factors for children's low academic performance. Tucker, Marx, and Long (1998) see family relocation as one cause of children's behavioral problems and poor school performance, and more so when the children live in single-parent households.

Long (2003) compared 65,000 children living in single-family homes with 921,000 children living in two-parent homes over an eight-year period. The study found that the children in single-parent homes were at greater risk for psychiatric disorders, alcohol-and narcotics-related diseases, and suicide.

Gender-related findings of Long's study indicated that boys in involuntarily created single-parent households are more prone to psychiatric diseases, alcohol-and drug-related illnesses, violence, and external injury, and have a 50% higher risk of death, while girls in the same situation are twice as likely to overdose on drugs or alcohol, or commit suicide. Noting that unemployment and lack of financial resources are sociological circumstances that sometimes cause these extreme consequences, the study concluded that separation and/or divorce present more dangers for children than a simple change in their living standard. In support of the above, Lipman (2002) found that children raised by single mothers were at greater risk for psychiatric and social difficulties and poor academic performance. These findings have been reported in both single-parent and two-parent households, but the statistics indicate that the degree to which the illnesses are present in children is significantly higher in single-parent households.

Consistent with Long's findings, Melton and Barry (1994) found that there is a strong relationship between low income and all categories of child abuse and neglect. According to Esau and Petermann (1999), depressive disorders are more common among young children and adolescents whose families have lower socioeconomic status and/or those whose parents are themselves depressed.

Depression is a common finding among women in single-parent households: one study reports 60% more admissions to psychiatric hospitals among women raising a family alone than among those with partners (Long, 2003). Depressed mothers who are the single adult responsible for children express loneliness, fear, insecurity, and financial problems (Schneller, 1976; Shaw, 1987), as well as feelings of being overwhelmed with the demands of parenthood, resulting in the perception of themselves as incompetent parents (Esau & Petermann, 1999). Women in single-parent households, whose spouses are imprisoned, sometimes experience so much despair, grief, stigma, and helplessness that they collapse under the strain, out of control and unable to communicate with their children (Shaw, 1987).

For their part, children in such households sometimes feel isolated and resist discipline from their mothers. They may respond by refusing to eat, or they may go so far as to commit a crime in the hope of reconnecting with their father within the judicial system that holds him prisoner. From the earliest studies through the most current, research clearly underscores the extensive ramifications of single parenting on children (Schneller, 1976).

# TRAUMA OF FAMILY SEPARATION/RELOCATION AND CULTURE SHOCK

It is well documented that the family members "left behind" by separation, divorce, or death undergo life-changing traumas and are at risk for multiple psychological illnesses and social upheaval. Research has also documented the equally traumatic changes suffered by those who are sent from a place where they are stable and rooted to an unfamiliar culture where they do not know the language and customs, have no ties and no way to start a new life. Involuntary departure of the kind that takes place either when an individual family member is deported or when an entire family leaves together in order to remain a unit, particularly when the exclusion is perceived as unjust, creates deportees/refugees who are subject to the experience of culture shock.

Ward, Bochner, and Furnham (2001) have integrated a number of research studies in relation to the psychology of culture shock. They cite five significant reasons refugees are the most disadvantaged of any groups forced to relocate:

1. The overwhelming stress they have been subjected to negatively affects their subsequent adjustment (Farias, 1991).

2. The risk of significant psychological and social adjustment issues increases because their migration is involuntary and largely motivated by "push" rather than "pull" factors (Kim, 1988; Mayada, 1983).

3. Their forced displacement is usually permanent, since, compared with immigrants and sojourners, refugees are far less likely to be able to return home (Beiser, Dion, Gotowiec, Hyman, & Vu, 1995; Majodina, 1989).

4. Those who leave a former home hurriedly, traveling lightly, are often ill-prepared for the societal changes they encounter, and are likely to be without sufficient economic resources to deal with life in a new culture. Vietnamese refugees, both adults and children, who had to make the decision to flee in only two days, found the relocation more difficult, in part because the nature of the displacement was both unanticipated and involuntary (Ekblad, 1993; Nicasso & Pate, 1984), forcing them to relocate without the benefits of language proficiency, financial resources, or survival skills (Boman & Edwards, 1984).

5. Their cultural backgrounds are often extremely different from those of the receiving countries (Stein, 1986), even those countries in the same general language/culture group.

## LIVING AS A REFUGEE

Living as a refugee, whether alone or as part of a family unit, is traumatic in the extreme. The multiple risk factors and stress generators associated with forced relocation have led one researcher to describe the refugee experience as a "social earthquake"(Mollica, 1990).

As would be expected, refugees exhibit more symptoms of psychological distress and psychological disorders than do members of the receiving society (Chu, 1972; Dube, 1968). For example, the neuroses levels of Chinese refugees newly arrived in Taiwan were found to be three times higher than those of native-born

Taiwanese (Chu, 1972), and exiled Namibians experience higher levels of anxiety when compared with residents of the receiving countries. A 1995 study of adolescent and young adult Afghanis living in the United States found that 29% met the criteria for major depression and 11% met the criteria for PTSD—the two most diagnosed conditions in refugees.

The sources of depression are numerous. For those who have been stripped of everything familiar and safe, homesickness, with its emphasis on the significance of the past compared with present suffering, is related to elevated levels of depression (Beiser et al., 1995), as are adjustment problems created by separation from family, memories of war, the difficulty of communicating with those in the home country, lack of job skills, and meager finances, to note just a few (Ekblad, 1993; Nicasso & Pate, 1984).

Specifically, refugee children have been shown to be at greater risk for alcohol abuse (Morgan, Wingard, & Felice, 1984), drug addiction (Amaral Dias, Vicente, Cabrita, & de Mendon, 1981) depression (Skhiri, Annabi, & Allani, 1982) and post-traumatic stress disorder (Sack, 1985).

It is possible there is a circumstance from which individuals who are exposed to grave injustice emerge completely unscathed. But a common theme in the research done for this study was that a perception of injustice accentuated the trauma. Even where there is no diagnosed trauma, this perceived injustice would seem to have negative cognitive and emotional effects.

# SYMPTOMOLOGY STEMMING FROM INJUSTICE-RELATED TRAUMA

Trauma that is coupled with injustice provokes symptomological reactions ranging from mild to severe; their duration can be short-lived or lifelong. Children exposed to early negative experience often re-create this trauma in their later lives (Harris, 2001).

When the U.S. government interned Japanese-Americans during WWII, the trauma did not stop with the parents. Indeed, Nagata (1993), referring to children whose parents were in the camps, observes: "The impact of the camp experience on the Sansei and for future generations is indisputable. Our parents suffered a humiliation which resulted in a denial of their very sense of identity, a denial which was passed on to their offspring" (Nagata, 1993, p. 53).

# DEPRESSION DEFINED

Depression is a common reaction to traumatic life events. Symptoms of depression are well documented and accepted within the professional community. Searching for the roots of late-life depression, Kraaij, Kremers, Arrensman, and Kerkhof (1998) found that prolonged negative life events such as chronic social difficulties, financial worries, separation from parents, relocation, physical illness in childhood, or being sentenced to jail show the highest correlation with depressive symptoms. The Surgeon General (*Mental Health: A Report of the Surgeon General*, 1999) added racism and discrimination as triggers for depression, and noted that groups at greater risk include women, unmarrieds, young people, African-Americans, and individuals with lower socioeconomic status.

The standard lists of depressive symptoms include:

- Feeling sad, blue, unhappy or "down in the dumps"
- Feeling tired, having little energy, unable to concentrate
- Feeling uneasy, restless or irritable
- Having trouble sleeping or eating (too little or too much)
- No longer enjoying previously pleasurable activities
- Loss of interest in sex or experiencing sexual difficulties
- Feeling that it takes longer than before to make decisions
- Feeling inadequate, like a failure, or unliked
- Feeling guilty without a rational reason, or putting oneself down
- Feeling that things always go or will go wrong, no matter how hard one may try (National Institute of Mental Health [NIMH], 1999/2001)

# ANXIETY DEFINED

Symptoms of anxiety have also been linked repeatedly to trauma. If one applies a continuum of symptomology to reactions to traumatic events, anxiety may be considered on the mild end of the continuum, while PTSD is at the severe end.

Symptoms of anxiety typically include:

- Excessive worrying

- Shortness of breath, palpitations, or shaking while at rest

- Fear of losing control or "going crazy"

- Avoidance of social situations because of fear

- Fears of certain objects, or of being in a place or situation where one feels there is no escape

- Feeling frightened of leaving home

- Recurring thoughts or images

- Compulsion to repeat behaviors

- Persistent reliving of an upsetting event from the past (NIMH, 1999/ 2001)

# PTSD DEFINED

PTSD is a debilitating condition that propels the sufferer to relive a traumatic experience again and again. While the definition of PTSD continues to evolve, there is a growing consensus around the requirements for diagnosis. The following definition is from the American Psychiatric Association, *Diagnostic and Statistical Manual of Mental Disorders* (2000):

> Post-traumatic stress disorder defines a specific syndrome in which trauma survivors are unable to clear their minds of the event. Three symptom clusters are associated with PTSD:
>
> 1) re-experienced distress from unwanted images, memories, nightmares or flashbacks of the event, with attendant physical symptoms such as palpitations, shortness of breath and other panic symptoms
> 2) avoidance of people, places or things associated with the trauma, coupled with emotional numbness, constriction or general unresponsiveness to the environment, and
> 3) hyperarousal, as reflected in physiological symptoms such as insomnia, irritability, impaired concentration, hypervigilance and increased startle responses. (*DSM-IV-TR*)

The existence of a small number of these symptoms is not sufficient to support a diagnosis of PTSD. Symptoms from all three clusters must be present. In addition, these symptoms must endure for at least one month and be so severe that the individual is substantially impaired socially, in the workplace, or in personal relationships.

The National Institute of Mental Health (1999/2001) found that PTSD in adulthood is more likely to be developed by those who have endured childhood abuse or other traumatic experiences. And while it was formerly believed that a shutdown of feelings was a healthy response to an experience of trauma, researchers currently see such emotional distancing as a possible precursor to PTSD.

Proximity to the traumatic event, being directly physically harmed or threatened, is no longer considered a necessary prerequisite for the appearance of symptoms of PTSD, although the *DSM* does not yet include proximity as a qualifier for a diagnosis of PTSD. Following September 11, 2001, studies comparing residents of lower Manhattan with residents of the entire New York City metropolitan area showed a higher prevalence of PTSD in those further away from the attacks on the World Trade Center. Two weeks after the attacks, the rates were 7.5% and 11.2%, respectively. Six months after the attacks, when the nation as a whole was studied, 3% was reported among New Yorkers, while the national rate was 5.8% (Silver, Holman, & McIntosh, 2002). So even when one is not the direct, or even nearby, "victim" of the traumatic event, the effect can still be significant.

The need for clarity and uniformity of guidelines makes it clear that the diagnosis of PTSD should not be assigned lightly. Unless there are fairly severe effects on an individual's quality of life, and the hallmark "flashback" or re-experiencing symptom, this diagnosis should be avoided in favor of other disorders, such as anxiety or depression.

# THE CONSTANT COMPARISON METHOD OF MEASURING EXPERIENCED TRAUMA AND PSYCHOLOGICAL SYMPTOMS

The constant comparison method which was used in this study combines both qualitative and quantitative techniques. Qualitative decisions, such as determining which symptoms are most common within a group of reports, must first be made. Results are then derived from tabulation and ordering according to quantity (Maykut & Morehouse, 1994).

First-person IIRAIRA-related traumatic injustices have been set down in text that is readily available to the researcher. Hundreds of stories, with their common elements, are capable of being codified, compared, and analyzed for meaning. All this can be accomplished without manipulation of interview subjects. Rather, the available data can be interpreted from the perspective of social psychology. This information must be organized and analyzed to extract meaningful information. The constant comparison method was used to analyze textual reports of experienced traumatic injustices.

According to Maykut and Morehouse (1994), "[t]he process of qualitative data analysis is fundamentally a nonmathematical analytical procedure that involves examining the meaning of people's words and actions" (p. 121).

Researchers using the constant comparison method must first explore and describe the phenomenon. This has already been partly accomplished in the case of IIRAIRA-related victims, whose stories are told in news accounts and self-reports. An examination of the material reveals patterns of description and content within the texts. While all the stories analyzed fall under the topic of IIRAIRA-affected individuals and families, the variety of nationalities, income levels, and locations indicated fulfills the inclusionary standard set by the constant comparison method.

Maykut and Morehouse (1994) describe four distinct steps necessary for constant comparison data analysis:

1.  Inductive category coding and simultaneous comparing of units of meaning across categories

2.  Refinement of categories

3.  Exploration of relationships and patterns across categories

4.  Integration of data, yielding an understanding of people and settings being studied

In the analysis, each category used can be demonstrated to have a specific rule for inclusion. For example, the category of "economic loss" should only be coded as present in the text when the text itself clearly states that the individual or family member has experienced loss of work, loss of transport, loss of housing, or some other material setback clearly related to economic position.

Categorical refinement of symptomology codes was guided by standard diagnostic tools: the Impact of Event Scale, the Hopkins Symptoms Checklist-25, and the *DSM-IV-TR*. From these reliable resources, a list of symptoms was produced. Key words indicative of such symptoms were added to the spreadsheet, and refined as the actual coding of units of meaning.

Exploration of relationships and patterns across categories included but was not limited to:

- Relationships between perceptions of injustice and frequency of reported symptoms

- Relationships between specific symptomology groupings indicative of particular diagnoses and other sociological coded units of meaning, such as economic, social, or cultural factors

Data integration followed the methodology outlined in Chapter 3.

After the words of individuals and family members affected by IIRAIRA were analyzed, codes were created and information categorized. Early inductive data analysis (pilot study) showed that the commonality observed in descriptions of circumstances, symptoms, and perceived injustice fits the qualifications for the constant comparison method, and is suitable for further analysis.

# 3

# *Methodology*

The purpose of this research was to explore the psychological and social impact of IIRAIRA on affected families.

The descriptive constant comparison study analyzed self-reported, post-1996 experiences and symptomology of 354 individuals who shared their stories on an Internet website devoted to IIRAIRA narratives. The 27 IIRAIRA-related stories from newspaper articles and 6 stories from a community hearing were incorporated to broaden the analysis.

## OVERVIEW OF THE CONSTANT COMPARISON STUDY

Two classes of information were analyzed for indications of psychological and social effects:

1. Self-reports from an IIRAIRA-related Internet web site

2. Reports extracted from text-based media accounts of IIRAIRA-affected families

The self-reports are located on a website titled "Stories from the Town Meeting" (http://www.ilw.com/micasa/tm.htm) (downloaded August 8, 2003), that is connected by a link to its host, a multi-services site called The Immigration Portal. The narrative texts used in this research were produced by site visitors who told of how

IIRAIRA has affected their lives. The stories are part of the website's archival data, and since there is minimal or no risk to the anonymous authors of this public information, informed consent was not needed. The complete archive of website stories was downloaded onto a hard drive and transferred intact onto an Excel spreadsheet, where a separate record was created for each narrative.

A number of journalistic stories were collected by an organization called "Citizens and Immigrants for Equal Justice" (CIEJ). Others are from a variety of print sources and from a community hearing at which witnesses told their IIRAIRA-related experiences under oath before a panel of experts. Some articles, with references, are archived at http://www.ciej.org/index.html.

Each record was examined first for validity. Did this particular narrative relate to TITLE III of IIRAIRA or to a different provision? The 1996 law deals with a number of other issues related to non-citizens, so if the story was not about an IIRAIRA-affected legal permanent U.S. resident being deported, it was marked invalid and discarded from the study.

A symptomology list, based on accepted diagnostic tools such as the Hopkins Symptom Checklist-25, Impact of Event Scale, and the *DSM-IV-TR*, was developed. After a preliminary review of the narratives, all included accounts were analyzed by noting key words, phrases, and other reasonably constructed textual indicators expressing IIRAIRA-related effects. Corresponding codes were then entered on the spreadsheet. Analyzing the frequency of the indicators' occurrence and their potential relationships produced a valid quantitative measurement for developing themes related to IIRAIRA effects; this measurement was then confirmed through the administration of a pilot study. Tables 1 and 2 contain sample spreadsheet information in a side-by-side comparison of the extracted symptom codes and some of the original unedited texts.

### Table 1
### IIRAIRA-Related Experienced Effects

| Related Effect(s) | Guide Words/Phrases from Stories |
| --- | --- |
| Perception of Injustice | Not fair; disproportionate punishment; breaking of cultural norms; wrong; I did not know about this law |
| Family Separation | Apart from spouse; not together anymore; won't see my children |
| Cultural Displacement | Don't know that place; never been there; don't know language; don't know anybody there |
| Economic Loss | Lost house, car, job |
| Arrest | Arrested in front of family; treatment while arrested and transported; humiliated |

## Table 1
### IIRAIRA-Related Experienced Effects (Continued)

| Related Effect(s) | Guide Words/Phrases from Stories |
|---|---|
| Custody | Separated from family; I was not able to see my family; INS abuses; housed with serious criminals; sent to a distant prison |
| Loss of Confidence in Legal System | Judges not able to help me; unfair judges; no money for attorney; no access to attorney |
| Positive Experience | Got rid of that spouse; my life is better now |

## Table 2
### IIRAIRA-Related Psychological Symptoms

| Related Symptom(s) | Guide Words/Phrases from Stories |
|---|---|
| Sadness | Crying, feeling blue, sad |
| Anger | I'm angry |
| Hopelessness/Help-lessness/Despair | No future; help me change this unjust situation |
| Loss of Control | Fear of losing control, "going crazy" |
| Loneliness | I feel alone |
| Lack of Energy | Tired; can't get going; slowed down; everything is an effort |
| Restlessness/Irritability | Snap at the kids; angry; frustrated; can't sit still |
| Sleep Disturbance | Can't sleep; sleep too much |
| Eating Disorders | Can't eat; eat too much; gained weight; lost weight |
| Loss of Pleasure | No interest in sex; previously pleasurable activities not wanted |
| Indecision/Lack of Concentration | Can't think; can't make up my mind; wander around; dazed |
| Sense of Failure | I'm a failure, useless |
| Guilt/Self-Blame | It's my fault |
| Worry | I'm worried |
| Recurring Thoughts | Always thinking about it; can't get it out of my head; thought about it when I didn't mean to |

Table 2
IIRAIRA-Related Psychological Symptoms (Continued)

| Related Symptom(s) | Guide Words/Phrases from Stories |
|---|---|
| Reliving the Event | It keeps going over and over in my head; I remember it all the time; it's like it happened all over again; flashbacks |
| Avoidance | Don't go where I used to; stay away from people/places |
| Physical Symptoms/ Anxiety | Difficulty breathing; shakes; palpitations; faintness; dizziness; weakness; headaches; trembling; pains, aches; health generally affected |
| Fear of Objects/Situations/Places | Fear of specific things, places related to trauma; people (police/INS officials) related to trauma; feeling fearful |
| Fear | Generalized fear; heightened arousal |
| Dread of the Outside World | Afraid to leave home |
| Startle Reaction | I'm jumpy/jittery; startled when phone rings, door knocks |
| Compulsive Behavior | Repetitive actions; stuck in a rut |
| Suicidal Thoughts/ Attempts | I think of dying; someone has died |
| Drug/Alcohol Abuse | Self or family members |

# PARTICIPANTS

All 185 quantitative study participants (152 website, 33 control data) conform to the IIRAIRA classification: they are legal permanent U.S. resident detainees, family members of a detainee who is in deportation proceedings or who has been deported, or parties connected to detainees/family members. A number of different countries are represented in the group of participants.

The pilot study confirmed that the text reports come from all over the country. A typical narrative is 500 words, and is not written to a professional standard. Some writers have limited English language skills, making certain reports difficult to understand. Still, each report was sufficiently clear that the researcher could make judgments regarding the appropriate codes for the narrative being analyzed.

# ETHICAL CONSIDERATIONS

Someone who reveals information in public forums such as the Internet, newspapers, and community hearings does not have a reasonable expectation of privacy. Therefore, even though the writers and/or subjects of the IIRAIRA-related stories have not expressly granted permission for them to be used in this study, it seems logical, given the gravity of the subject matter and the writers' expressed pleas for help, that they would welcome efforts to show the effects of this legislation on families. As with all post hoc analyses of this type, there was no opportunity for participant instruction, training, treatment, incentives, debriefing, or third-party verification of the stories.

# STUDY VARIABLES

Since the qualitative study was post hoc, and the website data to be analyzed had already been produced without study-related controls, there were no independent or dependent variables other than the simple test for validity: either IIRAIRA (TITLE III) or not IIRAIRA (TITLE III). Because the assumption can be made that stories from newspapers and the community hearing have been validated by their authors, such accounts serve as an independent check on the validity of the effects and symptoms reported in the website narratives.

The methodology chosen to examine the psychological and social effects of IIRAIRA, though the best available, was problematic. The primary difficulty lay in determining which codes to assign to which texts. Worry and fear are symptoms of depression and anxiety, respectively, according to the *DSM-IV-TR* and other symptomology guidelines. In the abstract, this seems clear-cut; in practice, given that each examined story has only a few lines of text, it is sometimes difficult to distinguish between the two symptoms. Most people use the terms interchangeably. Even more problematic for the researcher was how to categorize such terms as "afraid" and "worried." Which is fear, and which is worry? While every effort has been made to be consistent, it may not be possible to confidently assert that a text phrase belongs in one or the other category. This does not mean the information is too ambiguous to be useful. Rather it means that for similar symptoms and effects, less exact blanket categories may be more useful.

Similarly, a single text phrase such as "it's unfair" can be categorized in a number of ways. Obviously, this is an expression of the perception of injustice. But is it also an expression of anger? Sadness? Loss of confidence in the legal system? In this dissertation, such text phrases were assigned only to the most obvious category; however, text phrases that seemed strong enough to include other elements have been assigned to all the categories that apply. If all the "between the lines" information were to be somehow identified, extracted, and analyzed, the results could perhaps be more reflective of reality. But the categorization would become so subject to dispute as to be incapable of replication. So the researcher has opted for fairly conservative categorization, where most of the text phrases are very clearly appropriate.

The sample texts were written primarily by the female spouses of those incarcerated and deported because of IIRAIRA. The literature on depression clearly shows that women are more likely to demonstrate depressive symptoms than men. The lion's share of symptomology described by the authors involved depression. Is this because women are more cognizant of depression-like symptoms? As individuals directly affected by IIRAIRA, are they describing others' symptoms through the filter of their own experience, thereby skewing the results? If the majority of the authors were men, would there be more descriptions of anger or anxiety? Until a larger, more controlled study is conducted, these questions remain unanswered.

Similarly, the texts frequently do not specify exactly who is experiencing the symptoms or effects. Many texts simply say "we." Others alternate between describing the effects on the detainee and the effects on other family members. Most texts lump the effects together, since they involve the entire family.

The environment of the website where the stories were posted probably affected the authors in some measure. While the instructions for story submission seem relatively unbiased, the rest of the site offers visitors many overt and subtle clues, implying that their attitude toward IIRAIRA should be negative. Because this is an advocacy site, created and maintained by people who are opposed to IIRAIRA, it would be surprising if the authors' narratives were not influenced by this.

Additionally, if before writing their own stories the authors read those already on the site, their own narrative might be impacted. For example, most of the authors focus on the injustice of the law as it relates to the basic facts of their own case. A future study that does not depend on self-selected respondents who have an opportunity to read what others have written will be a more exact measure of the effects of IIRAIRA.

Finally, because a major portion of the researcher's data set originated on the Internet, there is no way to establish the absolute truthfulness of the narratives. Conceivably, a single individual could have written all of the stories. The authors could be lying. They may not even exist. Still, the fact that so many authors provided contact information, that the writing styles range from sophisticated to barely literate, and that the details differ even though the general themes are necessarily consistent suggests that these are real stories written individually by real people.

# STUDY LIMITATIONS

The pilot study revealed that if this research is to be reliably replicated, some symptoms needed further clarification; others needed to be combined because of their similarity.

**Hopelessness/Helplessness/Despair**, because their expressions overlapped, were better treated in combination. Especially signs of learned helplessness, appeals for help, expressions of non-physical pain, of enduring the pain in resigned silence, of being overwhelmed by the experience (one thing after another), of lack of confidence in the future: "No escape. Nothing we can do. No solution." Participants evaluate life as having no alternatives, no future. Negative evaluation of the future was key to the definition.

**Sadness** was used as a general category. It was coded when words such as "depressed, sad, cry, down" were used. Missing/longing for absent people (especially the detainee). This is a description of a current emotional state, perhaps as a result of an evaluation of hopelessness.

**Shock** expresses surprise, suddenness of arrest, usually associated with mention of arrest and immediate effect (cognitive dissonance): "unimaginable" "unexpected" "unbelievable." The date of arrest is immediately followed by an expression of extreme loss.

**Anger** was coded both when participants used the word "anger," and also when it was able to be inferred from the tone of the writing: defiant, sarcastic, agitated, unusually strong language to describe loss.

**Fear/Worry**, when they appeared in the text extract as these specific words, were coded as such, regardless of context/meaning. Defining these two symptoms so that they were clear and distinct from one another was very difficult. This problem was addressed by differentiating them from one another according to the strength of their effects on the participants. Worry causes an individual to ruminate, be concerned with, think about ramifications without actually committing to action or inaction. Fear seems more extreme and immediate. It causes one to commit to a course of action (I ran away from the bear) or to avoid a course of action (I didn't breathe because I feared the bear would hear me).

**Loneliness** was coded when expressions such as "I'm alone," "I miss him," or phrases relating to distance and longing were found in the text extracts.

**Loss of confidence** relates to mention of members of the legal profession in some uncomplimentary manner. Or refers specifically to a court incident, legal personnel, or legal procedure, in a manner that reflects the judgement that the incident disappointed them. This does not include mentions of law enforcement agents/agencies (arrest/custody), but only court procedures/administrations.

Allusions to large legal fees were entered in two categories: loss of confidence and economic loss.

## CRITERIA AND CRITERIA MEASURES

The reported effects of IIRAIRA were codified using a list that included psychological symptoms such as feelings of fear, and sociological experiences such as loss of goods and perception of injustice. While it was expected that most self-reports would be negative, the possibility that there would be some positive effects was also considered.

When an individual reported an IIRAIRA-related psychological or social effect, the researcher selected the appropriate code and entered it in the record alongside the narrative text so it could be checked for validity and reasonableness. Since this post hoc analysis relied on narratives written without a methodology for ensuring uniformity of reporting, a certain amount of judgment was used. For example, when a writer stated "this has destroyed my life," the researcher selected codes corresponding with the emotions typical of such a statement, such as helplessness, anger, sadness, frustration, etc.

Every time a symptom was reported in a narrative, it was coded. This coding simply shows that such symptomology was reported, not the degree or severity of the symptom. While it is tempting to extract information which could be used for scaling, perhaps showing, by gauging the intensity of their written reports, that some suffer more than others, the difficulties of coming to a uniform and reasonably consistent methodology are beyond the scope of this dissertation. Therefore, where a symptom was present, it was simply noted as present in the narrative and not described further or labeled as to intensity or duration.

For study reliability, the sample guided words used in analyzing the stories came from the stories themselves or from an accepted psychological term representing a wide range of meaning. For example, the phrase "disproportionate punishment" was used when a narrator expressed feeling severely punished, unjust punishment, hard consequences, and so forth.

Textual analysis and coding was conducted using the following rules:

1. Only IIRAIRA cases were valid. This required that the text itself describe the circumstances whereby IIRAIRA was invoked. Without this, a case was coded as invalid.

2. Only events directly associated with IIRAIRA were coded. An arrest or detention that took place prior to IIRAIRA was not recorded. Only the arrest/detention experience under IIRAIRA, where it was clearly traumatic or the author draws particular attention to the arrest or custody, was noted for this study.

3. Only events and symptoms described in the text as affecting either the detainee or family were recorded. Statements about the treatment or condition of a cellmate or another family are not recorded.

4. For an effect/symptom to be counted, it needed to merely be mentioned or referred to. The effect/symptom did not need to be explicit, though it should have been clear to the average reader.

5. If an effect or symptom was mentioned more than once within a case, even within a single sentence or phrase, it was counted multiple times. So, if a sentence contained six words specifying sadness, each of the six was entered in the sadness category.

6. After the initial coding, the data set was examined for consistency within coded areas. Text phrases judged to be more appropriate under different codes were moved. After all cases were reviewed for effects/symptoms, and the texts extracted and sorted, the data were examined to verify that all effect/symptom extracts were similar (justified for inclusion) or excluded as being non-conforming.

When all valid narratives had been analyzed and applicable codes recorded, the total scores for each effect and symptom were tallied and graphed as a percentage of responses that indicated a particular symptomology.

Testimony regarding perceptions of injustice was analyzed for possible relationship to the psychological and social effects of IIRAIRA-related experiences such as unexpected arrest, conditions of detention, ignorance of the law, legal costs/limitations, separation from family, loss of goods/employment, lifelong deportation to a country whose culture/language are unknown.

# STUDY DESIGN

This study relied on a post hoc analysis of self-reported symptomology resulting from an individual's exposure to IIRAIRA. Typically, Stories from the Town Meeting website contributors are IIRAIRA-affected family members whose loved one has been incarcerated and deported.

The following instructions are given to website visitors:

Stand up and speak your mind about the new law!

Tell us your story about how the IIRAIRA law has affected, or perhaps will affect, your life. When you finish, press the "submit" button at the bottom. Only what you write will be sent to us, nothing else! We have no way of tracing who you are or where you are, so feel free to say whatever you wish. On the other hand, if you do want to identify yourself, or receive news from us, simply go on to fill out the OPTIONAL RETURN FORM as well.

You are an: Immigrant, Lawyer, Concerned Citizen of the World, Concerned Family Member, Other

Enter your story or comments or suggestion in the space provided below:

In addition, visitors could have read the archive of previous stories before deciding to write their own anonymous stories, thereby coloring the perception of their experiences. In addition, individuals with favorable experiences under IIRAIRA would not be encouraged to tell their stories on such a site. In spite of the opportunity to remain anonymous, a large number of the authors of the main sample included their names and contact information, leading the researcher to believe that at least those stories are unlikely to have been made up.

There is no outside control over the maintenance of the website containing the information. Therefore, care was taken to eliminate self-reports that were judged invalid—that is, reports about any individuals not subjected to IIRAIRA. Valid stories were told by the individual directly affected, by a family member, or by a third party.

The narrative reports were not edited or changed by the researcher. Only the codes describing symptoms reported were used for the final analysis.

Maykut and Morehouse (1994) suggest using many photocopied sheets, but this study substituted a computer-generated spreadsheet and extensive copy/past-ing where it seemed more practical in the comparison of units of meaning across categories, thus providing a complete audit trail of the data.

Just two questions (Is this a valid record? What are the reported effects and symptoms?) were answered in the analysis of narratives used to gather information about the psychological and social effects produced by exposure to IIRAIRA.

# PROCEDURES CHECKLIST

1.  Data downloaded from web site, separated into individual stories

2.  Data organized to fit into spreadsheet

3.  Effects/symptoms data codes created

4.  Sample words developed through pilot study and anecdotal review

5.  Effects and symptoms developed through Hopkins Symptom Checklist-25, Impact of Event Scale, and the *DSM-IV-TR*

6.  Narratives read and symptomology data codes assigned for each valid record

7.  Data analyzed to find correlations and develop themes

8.  Pilot study of 25 stories refined key words and suggested the order of effects/symptoms so that more likely results were on top, easier to find

9.  Three hundred fifty-four stories reviewed from the Internet website, journalists, and a community hearing

10. Story authors noted: family/detainee/3rd party

11. Highlighted sufficient number of phrases, words, sentences within story to show the effect without referring to any other information; copied and pasted to table which matched effect/symptom code

12. Captured all multiple instances of effects/symptoms within a story, along with case number; attaching case numbers to text chunks allowed backward tracking of all texts so they could be referred to in context if needed for validity

13. Examined all text chunks assigned to an experience/symptom; inspected for uniformity and replicability; reassigned as needed

14. Transferred results to database, used database tools for enumeration, tallies, and comparison, leading to statistical analysis

# STATISTICAL DESIGN

The statistical design of this study is a simple analysis. Percentages were obtained after examining valid records that reported symptoms corresponding to those listed on the code table. After analyzing the frequency of self-reported symptomology compared to the total number of valid records, the researcher assigned a percentage score to each symptom. In the future, by comparing commonality of symptom code occurrence, a secondary analysis may indicate pairing or grouping of symptoms.

The data were also analyzed to identify possible relationships between perceptions of injustice and the presence of specific symptoms and symptom groupings. Reports of each of the effects were correlated with reports of each of the symptoms, and relationships between effects and symptoms were noted. The narrative reports were not edited or changed by the researcher. Only the codes describing effects or symptoms reported were used for the final analysis.

# 4

# *Results*

Results have been divided into four sections. The first section describes the sample, demographic information, and representativeness of the study. The second section describes coding standards. The third section is a qualitative one that uses the constant comparison method of analysis. It abstracts common categories, observations, and themes from website data, including quotations from the authors. The fourth section, which has been derived from the constant comparison method, is a quantitative one that expresses distribution of effects and symptoms in percentages and frequencies. This section generated hypotheses as the research evolved.

The hypotheses used chi-square tests to determine if variables were independent and if a difference existed. The first hypothesis stated that there was no difference between perception of injustice expressed by the group that reported one or more symptoms and the group that did not. The second hypothesis postulated no difference between symptoms experienced by family members and those experienced by detainees. The third hypothesis posited no difference between effects self-reported on the web and those in the data collected from the community hearing and published articles. The fourth hypothesis sought to find no difference between symptoms self-reported on the web and those in the data obtained from the community hearing and published articles.

## DESCRIPTION OF THE SAMPLE

The study employed three samples. The main sample of 354 individual website postings yielded 152 valid IIRAIRA-related stories. The two control samples were drawn from journalistic accounts (articles) about IIRAIRA detainees and their families, and from the transcript of a 1999 videotaped community hearing sponsored by the American Friends Service Committee. Of the 27 stories found in the articles, 19 were valid for the study. Of the 10 stories from the community hearing, 6 were valid for the study.

# DEMOGRAPHIC INFORMATION

Website stories in the main sample were written by self-selected individuals who voluntarily posted accounts of their experiences with IIRAIRA. Eighty-two percent of the web authors are family members of detainees; the vast majority of them are female spouses. Thirteen percent are the detainees themselves and about 5% are third parties not related to the detainees (Table 3).

Stories were rated as valid or invalid based on the circumstances surrounding detention and/or deportation. Of 354 stories in the main sample, 152 were valid. Invalid stories were noted as invalid, and were excluded from the study.

### Table 3
### Web Stories Distributed by Author

| Web Author | Stories | % |
|---|---|---|
| Family Member | 124 | 82 |
| Detainee | 20 | 13 |
| Third Party | 8 | 5 |
| Total | 152 | 100 |

There were no dropouts from the study, since the nature of the research did not require any additional participation beyond what the subjects (self-selected individuals who visited the website) had already provided.

Three of the main sample stories were valid IIRAIRA accounts but were not included in this research either because of brevity or because the website authors did not describe experiences or symptoms relevant to the scope of this study. For example, story #166 says: "November 8, 1998 My wife is in hearings now and sh has been here since 1969."

# REPRESENTATIVENESS

No type of random sampling was imposed; participants were self-selected. The main sample included only individuals who are literate, have basic computer skills, understand English, were able to find the website, and were inspired to write their story. Members of this self-selected group had the option of remaining anonymous.

Only individuals willing to speak with journalists were included in the journalistic sample, and only individuals who were willing to speak in a public forum were included in the community hearing sample. There has been no third-party verification of any of these accounts. The journalists were presumed to have adhered to journalistic standards regarding the veracity of the articles. Community hearing speakers testified under oath.

The website instructs visitors to "enter your story or comments or suggestions in the space provided below." However, it is possible that before deciding to write an account, visitors can scan the archive of stories previously entered on the site, thereby potentially affecting the perception of their own experiences. In addition, individuals whose IIRAIRA-related experiences are favorable would not be encouraged to tell their stories on such a site.

In spite of the opportunity to remain anonymous, a large number of authors included names and contact information, leading to the assumption, when assessing veracity, that those stories, at least, were unlikely to have been fabricated.

The inclusion of the journalistic and community hearing stories was intended to act as a control/check on the data from the web self-reports.

# CODING STANDARDS

The primary challenge in the study was to codify the text phrases correctly and consistently. Ambiguities within the texts were common, as were vocabulary-related inconsistencies and errors. In theory, "sadness" seems straightforward nomenclature; in practice it was very difficult to determine which text phrases were clearly indicative of sadness and which may have represented a similar symptom.

Ultimately, there can be no completely accurate method for coding this type of information. However, the most consistent methods available were employed throughout the study.

After the initial coding, the texts were compared. If all the text phrases assigned a specific code were similar, it was determined that enough consistency had been achieved to use the data for analysis. While any individual text phrase may legitimately be challenged, the totality of the data were judged sufficient to derive useful results.

# QUALITATIVE FINDINGS

Since individual website narratives often include multiple effects and symptoms, some story excerpts were tabulated in more than one category.

## *Effects*

Clearly, the highest percentages in the study were in the category labeled perception of injustice. The authors' reports varied widely, but the following examples, taken verbatim from the website, are indicative of the common use of explicit judgments.

> 321—The 1996 law is harsh and discriminates against immigrants

> 345—This is an obviuos violation of the human rights

> 348—Please continue our fight against the unconstitutional law

Another commonly expressed sentiment related to the totality of the losses experienced and the magnitude of the extent to which lives have been altered.

> 002—I have lost everything due to these laws

> 321—he was sentencing himself to a what now amounts to a "life" sentence

IIRAIRA's unconstitutionality and the unfairness of retroactivity were commonly cited as adversities. Many authors expressed a belief that this law was enacted to specifically and unjustly single out immigrants for inequitable punishment. These perceptions of injustice were evident in frequent references to violations of the constitution, lack of respect for family integrity, and denial of judicial review. Words such as "un-American" and "unfair" were often used. Authors who have U.S. citizen family members emphasized that the unjust effects of the law go far beyond the legal permanent resident community, impacting the whole of society.

> 086—I can not believe that this is happening in America

> 307—but my human and civil rights as a United States citizen will be violated to the extreme

> 313—THIS IS NOT AMERICAN

Another component of the perception of injustice category was the "call to action" voiced in texts that explicitly challenged IIRAIRA.

310—We must stop these injustices

325—This draconian law should be changed

332—There should be something done in reference to this new 1996 law that is hurting many, many, people, families and children

Family separation and cultural displacement were among the most burdensome and distressing concerns mentioned by the authors. Specifically, family separation worries tended to focus on the negative effects on minor children, while cultural displacement anxieties included language barriers, length of time away from the country of origin, and threats to health and safety in the country of origin.

002—My children are so lost right now, and asking for there father everyday

029—I HAVE TO FACE MY CHILDREN EVERYDAY WITH THE QUESTION OF WHEN THEIR FATHER WILL BE HOME

048—The separation from him and his daughter may be unbearbale to both parties

068—fear, fear because I worry that I will not see my mother again

048—Not knowing the language and culture of people in Jordan

053—find herself destitute and homeless in a country she never knew

059—The United States is the only country he knows. He has never left this country since he entered. He went to day care, grammar school, high school, and graduated college in this country.

113—If my husband is sent back to Somalia he may be killed

241—He has been in this country since he was 10 years old and has not lived in Mexico for almost 20 years

Expressions of loss of confidence in the legal system were similar to those in the perception of injustice category, with the addition of a specific focus on the system's procedures and personnel.

> 008—HAVE ASKED MY HUSBAND LAWYER TO TRY AN GET MY HUSBAND OUT ON BAIL BUT THEY SAID NO

> 027—A district attorney in Cabarrus County was asked if she could help get the charge reduce to keep him from being deported and she replied absolutely not, and stated this would be a better area if they were all deported

> 164—I went to the hearing and do not even know why the gov't provides them, their minds are already made up and these so called "INS judges" do not take anything into consideration.

Economic loss was identified in statements of financial distress directly related to the effects of IIRAIRA on the family as a whole. Commonly mentioned were legal expenses, loss of the detained spouse's income, loss of automobile and/or house, and inability to support the children.

> 005—sinc!††e then i have lost my job, my car, i cannot find work since the ins has taken all my paper work

> 025—have car loans, credit cards and personal line loans that I can never pay all in one shot

> 029—STRUGGLE EVERYDAY AS A MOTHER ALONE TO FEED AND CLOTHES MY CHILDREN

> 054—We have been ripped off by attorneys

> 059—We are loosing every thing we worked so hard for

Reports relating to custody were of two general kinds. Some factual reports simply listed the times, dates, and locations of custody, and included the information that detainees are moved frequently. Others spoke more emotionally of abuses experienced in custody. When a writer's country of origin has no diplomatic relationship with the U.S., an author may have mentioned that this results in a "life sentence" of detention in this country.

> 002—took him to the sherrif dept. and he is still there

> 008—THEY MOVE HIM FOUR TIMEs

125—Currently he is being detained in Gadsden, Alabama, the third jail he has been to since his apprehension by INS officials in January. They have treated him worse than a terrorist

137—We cannot even visit him

312—Due to the fact that Cuban's are not returned to their country, Raulis being detained as a "lifer"

Reports of arrest tended to focus on the circumstances of the arrest itself, detailing how traumatic it was for the detainee, the family, and/or witnesses.

005—i was then shackled, cuffed and driven to an airfield in up state new york and flown to the federal detention center for another two weeks.

105—ONE DAY I CAME BACK HOME FROM WORK AND TWO MANS WERE WAITING FOR ME OUT SIDE MY HOUSE, THEY SHOW ME THERE CREDENTIALS AND I AGREE TO GO TO IMMIGRATION OFICCE NOT KNOING I WILL BE DEPORTED THE VERY NEXT DAY

147—I waited, and waited for him to get home. The time kept passing by. Finally I a phone call from him telling me that he had been arrested and was going to jail

339—I had returned home from work only to find my husband gone

## Symptoms

Most of the stories contained text which was clearly and easily identified as an explicit description of symptomology. Of these, expressions of helplessness, hopelessness, despair, sadness, anger and shock were the most common. Many authors included appeals for help, and these were tabulated in the "helpless/hopeless" category.

Hopelessness, helplessness, and despair were virtually indistinguishable in the texts, and so were assigned the same code. Common among the texts were pleas for help, as well as expressions of despair and lack of hope for the future.

005—I HAVE TRUELY BEEN SENTENCED TO DEATH

027—Please help save my childrens father an my fiancée

253—There are no words that can accurately express how hopeless and devistated I feel to lose my best friend of 20 years

317—i sow my wife tears coming down her face and my kid's didn't know wether to kry or to stik ther fingers thru the small opening of the glass

323—How will we ever make it through this

Sadness was characterized in the stories by expressions of negative emotional effect. Sometimes the explanation was clear, as when it described the tears of a child. Other descriptions of sorrow were less explicit but still clear indications of sadness. Interestingly, these descriptions focused more frequently on family members, such as minor children, than on the author's feelings.

029—THE LOOK AND TEARS OF A 9 YEAR OLD DAUGHTER KNOWING THAT HER DAD WOULD BE MISSING HER TENTH BIRTHDAY

068—This has caused my family a lot of pain and tears

312—it breaks my heart to see him be locked up

348—She is very depressed

Anger was expressed as antagonism or rage toward the cause of the injury. In the stories, it was the government and its institutions toward which the authors directed their anger. One author (#175) even made plain his belief that "this is how terrorists are born."

038—Me and my family are so upset with the United State government

105—MY LITTLE JOSH HAD SED THAT WHEN HE GROW'S UP HE WILL BET UP THE PEAPLE WHOM TOOK ME A WAY!!!

119—Is this America?? Does anyone at INS have a clue as to what the statue of liberty stands for??

173—am going through hell!!!

Several authors reported the symptom of shock/surprise in general terms, while others described very specifically the trauma associated with the arrest of a family member.

091—picked up from his home early in the morning as he was going to work in front of his wife and children by police officers and INS officers. He was hancuffed and treated as a criminal. We were all in shock because he had not committed any crime and now was being detained.

163—I lived the nightmare of having my husband and my children's father taken from us

Expressions of fear indicated the web authors' awareness of actual or threatened danger. Many used the word "fear" or "scared" in their texts.

074—I now live under siege of fear for the past five years

091—picked up from his home early in the morning as he was going to work in front of his wife and children by police officers and INS officers. He was hancuffed and treated as a criminal. We were all in shock because he had not committed any crime and now was being detained.

173—on our return home he was detained at Kennedy airport-humiliated, and scared to death

349—It is laws and circumstances like this that have created the overwhelming number of homeless on the streets, and I fear that soon I will be one of them

Verbalizing a loss of control showed that an author was either worried on a personal level or that he/she observed another affected person who was similarly unable to maintain control of his/her life and actions.

029—MAKE PHONE CALLS LIKE A MANIAC NOT KNOW!††ING WHEN I WOULD SEE MY HUSBAND AGAIN

119—I'm going crazy

320—I think I'm having a nervous breakdown

Some authors reported disrupted sleep patterns: sleeping too much, not sleeping enough, waking up throughout the night.

163—At times I still have sleepless nights thinking about what we went through

314—I often loose sleep questioning how am I going to win this

Suicidal thoughts were clearly expressed. Authors reported thoughts of killing themselves in order to escape from the pain of the situation.

315—and he feels very isolated, bordering on suicidal

317—she whant it to just take some pills and forget about it

A sense of failure manifests itself in only one case studied.

317—when i read this in my commmpiuter i felt soo worth less

A lack of energy was verbalized in only one case.

175—self................very angry††hungry, angry, lonley and tired

# DESCRIPTIVE STATISTICS

Most stories included one or more accounts of effects and symptoms. Table 4 shows that out of 152 valid cases, 146 reported effects and 107 reported symptoms.

On average, each story reported 5.2 effects and 2.3 symptoms. Of the 152 valid stories, 117 (77%) reported perception of injustice, making it the most prevalent effect of IIRAIRA in this study. Family separation ranked second, with 68 (45%) stories reporting. Cultural displacement was ranked third, with 59 (39%) stories reporting. Loss of confidence in the legal system and economic loss both ranked fourth, with 49 (32%) stories reporting. The category of custody ranked fifth, with 44 reported stories (29%). The category of arrest ranked last, with 36 (24%).

**Table 4**
*Valid and Invalid Web Stories/Stories with Effects and Symptoms*

| Web Story Breakdowns | Number | % |
|---|---|---|
| Total number of web stories examined | 354 | |
| Stories found to be invalid | 202 | 57 |
| Total valid stories | 152 | 43 |
| | | |
| Stories w/reported effects | 146 | 96 |
| Stories w/reported symptoms | 107 | 70 |

Table 5 and Figure 1 illustrate the frequency and percentage of stories reporting effects.

### Table 5
### *Frequency and Percentage of Reported Effects*

| Reported Effects | Frequency | % |
|---|---|---|
| Perception of injustice | 117 | 77 |
| Separation of family | 68 | 45 |
| Cultural displacement | 59 | 39 |
| Loss of confidence in legal system | 49 | 32 |
| Economic loss | 49 | 32 |
| Custody | 44 | 29 |
| Arrest | 36 | 24 |
| Positive feeling | 0 | 0 |

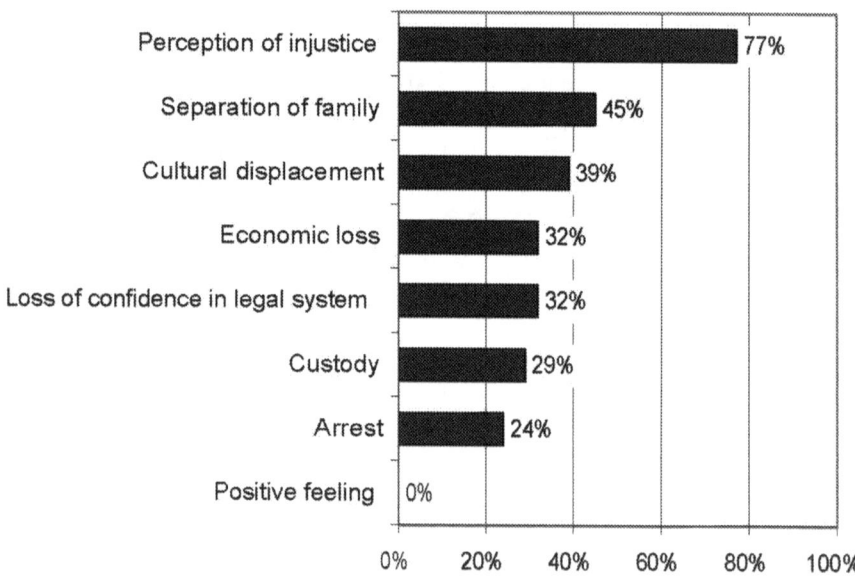

*Figure 1.* Percentage of stories reporting effects.

Most of the stories reported one or more symptoms. The most common was hopelessness/despair: 60 (39%) of the 152 valid stories reported one or more occurrences of this symptom; 40 (26%) expressed sadness. Anger was reported in 27 (18%), and shock/surprise followed closely with 25 (16%). Fear and indecision/lack of concentration were reported in 22 and 21 (14%) of the stories, and worry in 17 (11%). Fear of objects/situations/places was reported in 12 (8%); the same number, 12 (8%), reported loneliness. Loss of control was reported in 7 (5%). Shame/guilt and sleep disturbance were each described in 4 (3%), followed by lack of energy and physical symptoms/anxiety in 3 (2%). Avoidance and suicidal thoughts were each reported in 2 (1%) of the stories.

It should also be noted that none of the website authors mentioned the following symptoms specifically, by name: restlessness/irritability, loss of pleasure, sense of failure, recurring thoughts, eating disorders, reliving the event, dread of the outside world, startle reaction, compulsive behavior, or drug/alcohol abuse.

Table 6 and Figure 2 illustrate the frequency and percentage of multiple instances of reported symptoms.

Distribution of the 793 effects and 355 symptoms reported across stories was similar to that within stories. Table 7 lists the distribution of reported effects in terms of frequency. The most often reported was perception of injustice (318 times), accounting for a full 40% of the total of 793 reported effects. Second most frequently reported was separation of family (116 times), accounting for 15%. Cultural displacement ranked third, with 105, which is 13% of reported effects. Economic loss ranked fourth, with 79 (10%), followed by custody, with 69 (9%).

Table 7 and Figure 3 illustrate the distribution of multiple instances of reported effects in terms of percentages. Each report of an effect within a story was counted as a single event; therefore, multiple reports of a given effect within the same story were counted as multiple events.

**Table 6**
*Frequency and Percentage of Reported Symptoms*

| Reported Symptoms | Frequency | % |
|---|---|---|
| Hopelessness/Despair | 60 | 39 |
| Sadness | 40 | 26 |
| Anger | 27 | 18 |
| Shock/Surprise | 25 | 16 |
| Fear | 22 | 14 |
| Indecision/Lack of concentration | 21 | 14 |
| Worry | 17 | 11 |
| Fear of objects/situations/places | 12 | 8 |
| Loneliness | 11 | 7 |
| Loss of control | 7 | 5 |
| Shame/Guilt/Self-blame | 4 | 3 |
| Sleep disturbance | 4 | 3 |
| Lack of energy | 3 | 2 |
| Physical symptoms/Anxiety | 3 | 2 |
| Avoidance | 2 | 1 |
| Suicidal thoughts/Attempts | 2 | 1 |
| Restlessness/Irritability | - | 0 |
| Loss of pleasure | - | 0 |
| Sense of failure | - | 0 |
| Recurring thoughts | - | 0 |
| Eating disorders | - | 0 |
| Reliving the event | - | 0 |
| Dread of the outside world | - | 0 |
| Startle reaction | - | 0 |
| Compulsive behavior | - | 0 |
| Drug/alcohol abuse | - | 0 |

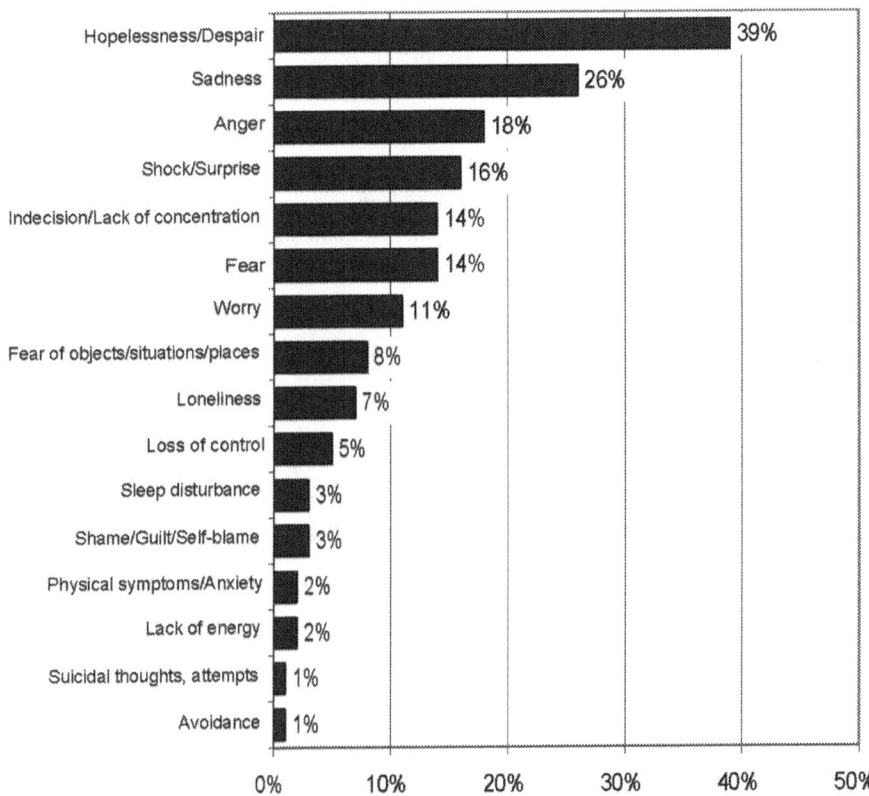

*Figure 2.* Percentage of stories reporting symptoms.

**Table 7**
*Frequency and Percentage of Multiple Reported Effects*

| Reported Effects | Frequency | % |
|---|---|---|
| Perception of injustice | 318 | 40 |
| Separation of family | 116 | 15 |
| Cultural displacement | 105 | 13 |
| Economic loss | 79 | 10 |
| Custody | 69 | 9 |
| Loss of confidence in legal system | 66 | 8 |
| Arrest | 40 | 5 |
| Positive feelings | - | 0 |
| Total | 793 | 100 |

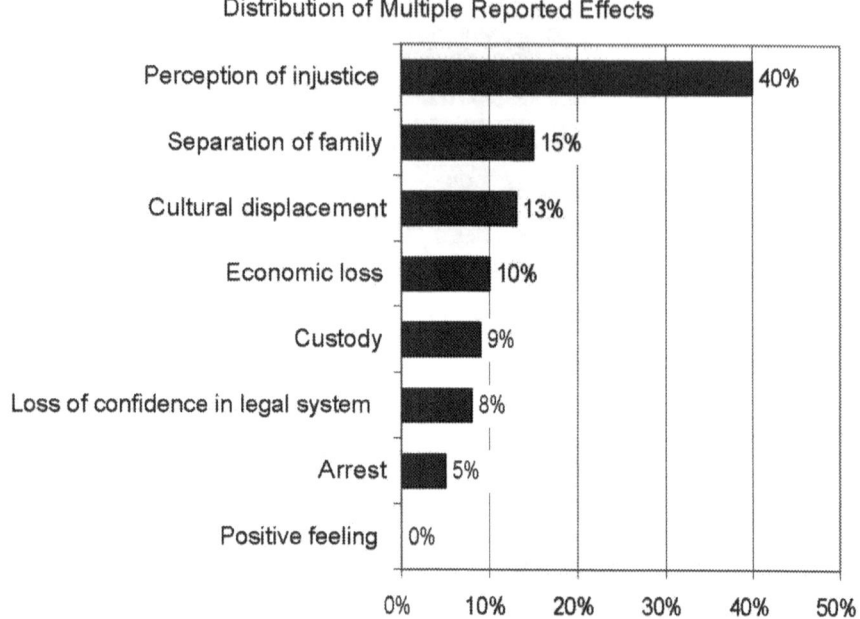

*Figure 3.* Percentage distribution of multiple reported effects.

Table 8 shows the distribution of all reported symptoms. As was noted in Table 6 and Figure 2, hopelessness/despair was the most prevalent symptom reported, with a frequency of 94, accounting for 26% of the 355 total symptoms reported. Sadness was reported 55 times (15%). Shock/surprise was reported 37 times (10%), followed by anger 31 times (9%). Fear and indecision/lack of concentration were each reported 27 times (8%). Worry was reported 23 times (6%). Loneliness, reported 18 times, and fear of objects/situations/places, reported 16 times, each represented 5% of the symptoms tabulated. Loss of control represented 2% of the total, and shame/guilt/self-blame, sleep disturbance, lack of energy, avoidance, physical symptoms/anxiety and suicidal thoughts/attempts each represented 1% of the total symptoms reported.

Table 8
*Frequency and Percentage of Multiple Reported Symptoms*

| Reported Symptoms | Frequency | % |
|---|---|---|
| Hopelessness/Despair | 94 | 26 |
| Sadness | 55 | 15 |
| Shock/Surprise | 37 | 10 |
| Anger | 31 | 9 |
| Fear | 27 | 8 |
| Indecision/Lack of concentration | 27 | 8 |
| Worry | 23 | 6 |
| Loneliness | 18 | 5 |
| Fear of objects/Situations/Places | 16 | 5 |
| Loss of control | 7 | 2 |
| Shame/Guilt/Self-blame | 4 | 1 |
| Sleep disturbance | 4 | 1 |
| Lack of energy | 3 | 1 |
| Avoidance | 3 | 1 |
| Physical symptoms/Anxiety | 3 | 1 |
| Suicidal thoughts/Attempts | 3 | 1 |
| Restlessness/Irritability | - | 0 |
| Loss of pleasure | - | 0 |
| Sense of failure | - | 0 |
| Recurring thoughts | - | 0 |
| Eating disorders | - | 0 |
| Reliving event | - | 0 |
| Dread of the outside world | - | 0 |
| Startle reaction | - | 0 |
| Compulsive behavior | - | 0 |
| Drug/Alcohol abuse | - | 0 |
| Total | 355 | 100 |

Figure 4 illustrates the distribution of reported symptoms in terms of percentages.

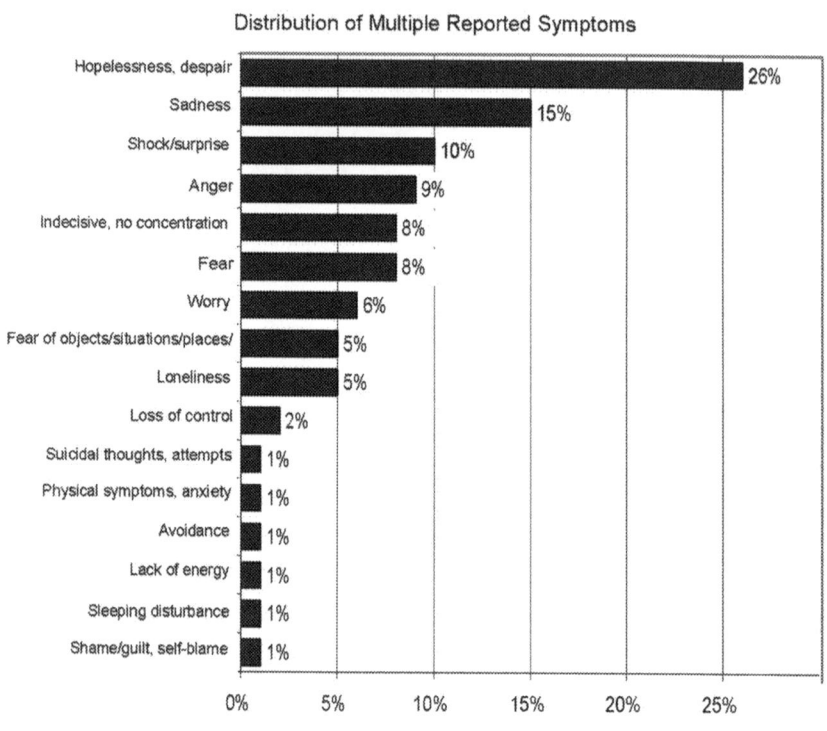

*Figure 4.* Percentage distribution of multiple reported symptoms.

# CORRELATIONS BETWEEN VARIABLES

A linear correlation between all reported effects and symptoms indicated a number of notable relationships among the variables.

The data set revealed that there is a significant relationship between the symptoms of hopelessness/despair and indecision/lack of concentration, $r = .54$, $p = .01$. There was also a significant relationship between the symptoms of worry and fear of objects/situations/places, $r = .56$, $p = .01$.

The data suggested the existence of a number of moderate relationships between effects and symptoms. The first of these is between the effect of arrest and the symptom of shock/surprise, $r = .04$, $p = .01$. The second is between the effect of separation of family and the symptom of sadness, $r = .46$, $p = .01$.

Other moderately strong relationships occurred between different symptoms. Fear and fear of objects/situations/places were significantly associated, $r = .42$, $p = .01$. Shame/guilt/self-blame and suicidal thoughts/attempts were significantly correlated, $r = .44$, $p = .01$.

Among the weaker relationships, three are between an effect and a symptom. First, the data identified an association between the effect of loss of confidence in the legal system and the symptom of hopelessness/despair, $r = .33$, $p = .01$. Second, the effect of separation of family is also related to the symptom of hopelessness/despair, $r = .31$, $p = .01$. Third, the effect of separation of family is related to the symptom of loneliness, $r = .31$, $p = .01$.

Additional weak relationships were identified between pairs of symptoms: sadness and shame/guilt/self-blame, $r = .34$, $p = .01$; loneliness and fear, $r = .36$, $p = 0.00$; loneliness and lack of energy, $r = .30$, $p = .01$; and between a pair of effects: arrest and custody, $r = .31$, $p = .01$.

Table 9 lists the relationships between some variables, the number of reported instances of the variables, and the linear correlation coefficient between the two.

A complete table of correlations among the variables is attached as Appendix A.

# HYPOTHESIS TESTING

The first hypothesis tested whether individuals who self-reported IIRAIRA-related symptomology perceived their situation to be unjust. Of the 117 cases that reported the effect of perception of injustice, 85 (63%), also reported symptoms. Of the 35 cases that did not report the effect of perception of injustice, 22 (53%) reported symptoms. This means that perception of injustice was higher among those who also reported symptoms than it was among those who did not. This result conformed with the literature that predicted a relationship between the perception of injustice and the severity or intensity of emotional affect. The following test examines whether or not this difference could be due to random variation:

$H_0$: There is no difference in occurrences of reports of perception of injustice between stories that report symptoms and those that do not.

$H_1$: There is a difference in occurrences of reports of perception of injustice between stories that report symptoms and those that do not (see Table 10).

### Table 9
#### Correlations Between Variables

| Correlations | Correlation Coefficient | p Value | n |
|---|---|---|---|
| Significant Relationships (Symptom to Symptom) | | | |
| Hopelessness/Despair Indecision/Lack of concentration | 0.54 | .01 | 60 |
| Worry Fear of objects/Situations/Places | 0.56 | .01 | 21 |
| Moderate Relationships (Effect to Symptom) | | | |
| Arrest Shock/Surprise | 0.40 | .01 | 45 |
| Separation of family Sadness | 0.46 | .01 | 82 |
| Moderate Relationships (Symptom to Symptom) | | | |
| Fear Fear of objects/Situations/Places | 0.42 | .01 | 26 |
| Shame/Guilt/Self-blame Suicidal thoughts/Attempts | 0.44 | .01 | 5 |
| Weak Relationships (Effect to Symptom) | | | |
| Loss of confidence in legal system Hopelessness/Despair | 0.33 | .01 | 79 |
| Separation of family Hopelessness/Despair | 0.31 | .01 | 93 |
| Separation of family Loneliness | 0.31 | .01 | 69 |
| Weak Relationships (Symptom to Symptom) | | | |
| Sadness Shame/Guilt/Self-blame | 0.34 | .01 | 41 |
| Loneliness Fear | 0.36 | .01 | 29 |

## Table 9
### Correlations Between Variables (Continued)

| Correlations | Correlation Coefficient | p Value | n |
|---|---|---|---|
| Loneliness Lack of energy | 0.30 | .01 | 11 |
| Weak Relationships (Effect to Effect) | | | |
| Arrest Custody | 0.31 | .01 | 61 |

## Table 10
### Hypothesis 1 Results

| Observed | PI* | No PI* | Sum |
|---|---|---|---|
| Stories with reported symptoms | 85 | 22 | 107 |
| Stories without reported symptoms | 32 | 13 | 45 |
| Sum | 117 | 35 | 152 |
| **Expected** | **PI*** | **No PI*** | **Sum** |
| Stories with reported symptoms | 82 | 25 | 107 |
| Stories without reported symptoms | 35 | 10 | 45 |
| Sum | 117 | 35 | 152 |

*Note.* Degrees of freedom = 1; significance level = 0.05; critical value = 3.84; chi-square = 1.24. PI = perception of injustice; No PI = no perception of injustice.

Since the chi-square of 1.24 was less than the critical value of 3.84, the distributions were not significantly different at the .05 level. We could not reject the null hypothesis, and we therefore could determine that there was no difference in occurrences of reports of perception of injustice between stories that reported symptoms and those that did not.

The second hypothesis sought to test whether there was a difference in the types of symptoms reported by families and those reported by detainees. Families reported a total of 282 symptoms and detainees reported a total of 59. Figure 5 illustrates the distribution in terms of total symptoms reported for each.

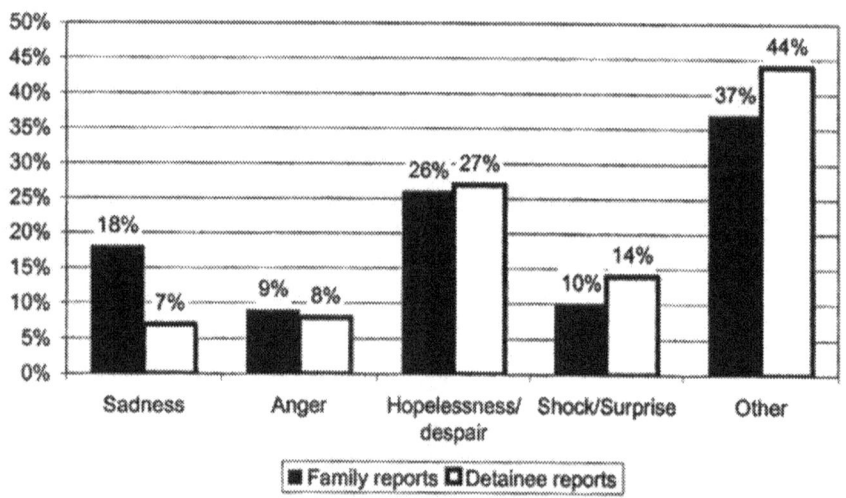

*Figure 5.* Distribution of symptoms reported by detainees and families.

$H_0$: Detainees report the same types of symptoms as do the families.

$H_1$: Detainees report different types of symptoms than do the families (see Table 11).

### Table 11
### *Hypothesis 2 Results*

| Observed | Sadness | Anger | Hopelessness/ Despair | Shock/ Surprise | Other | Sum |
|---|---|---|---|---|---|---|
| Family reports | 51 | 26 | 74 | 28 | 103 | 282 |
| Detainee reports | 4 | 5 | 16 | 8 | 26 | 59 |
| Total | 55 | 31 | 90 | 36 | 129 | 341 |

| Expected | Sadness | Anger | Hopelessness/ Despair | Shock/ Surprise | Other | Sum |
|---|---|---|---|---|---|---|
| Family reports | 45.48 | 25.6 | 74.4 | 29.8 | 107 | 282 |
| Detainee reports | 9.516 | 5.36 | 15.6 | 6.23 | 22.3 | 59 |
| Total | 55 | 31 | 90 | 36 | 129 | 341 |

*Note.* Degrees of freedom = 4; significance level = 0.05; critical value = 9.49; chi-square = 5.25.

The chi-square of 5.25 was less than the critical value of 9.49 required to reject the null hypothesis at a 5% level of significance. There was no significant difference in the types of symptoms reported by families and by detainees.

## Reported Symptoms Relative to Standard Symptoms List

In order to interpret study data associated with symptoms of depression, PTSD and anxiety, a relativity list was compiled from diagnostic tools such as the Hopkins Symptom Checklist-25, Impact of Event Scale, and the *DSM-IV-TR*. Table 12 illustrates the connection between reported symptoms and the three conditions.

Table 12

*Reported Symptoms as Indicators of the Conditions of Depression, Anxiety, and PTSD*

|  | Symptoms | Depression | Anxiety | PTSD |
|---|---|---|---|---|
| S1 | Sadness | * |  |  |
| S2 | Anger |  |  |  |
| S3 | Hopelessness/Despair | * |  | * |
| S4 | Loss of control |  | * |  |
| S5 | Shock/Surprise |  |  | * |
| S6 | Loneliness | * |  |  |
| S7 | Worry |  | * |  |
| S8 | Fear |  | * | * |
| S9 | Lack of energy | * |  |  |
| S10 | Restlessness/Irritability |  | * |  |
| S11 | Loss of pleasure | * |  |  |
| S12 | Indecision/Lack of concentration | * |  | * |
| S13 | Sense of failure | * |  |  |

**Table 12**
*Reported Symptoms as Indicators of the Conditions of Depression, Anxiety, and PTSD* (Continued)

|  | *Symptoms* | *Depression* | *Anxiety* | *PTSD* |
|---|---|:---:|:---:|:---:|
| S14 | Shame/Guilt/Self-blame | * |  |  |
| S15 | Recurring thoughts |  | * | * |
| S16 | Eating disorders | * |  |  |
| S17 | Sleep disturbance | * | * | * |
| S18 | Reliving event |  |  | * |
| S19 | Avoidance |  |  | * |
| S20 | Physical symptoms/Anxiety |  | * |  |
| S21 | Fear of objects/situations/places/ |  | * |  |
| S22 | Dread of the outside world |  | * |  |
| S23 | Startle reaction |  |  | * |
| S24 | Compulsive behavior |  | * |  |
| S25 | Suicidal thoughts/attempts | * |  |  |
| S26 | Drug/alcohol abuse | * | * | * |

Key: * = condition corresponding to the symptom.

A considerable number of stories reported symptoms associated with depression and PTSD. Significantly, 28% of all stories reported two or more different symptoms of depression, while 8% reported three or more and 3% reported four or more. An almost equal number of stories reported different symptoms of PTSD: 29% reported two or more different symptoms, 8% reported three or more, and 1% reporting four or more. Symptoms of anxiety were less frequent, with only 12% of stories reporting two or more different symptoms, and 3% reporting three or more, and 1% reported four or more. These findings are illustrated in Table 13.

### Table 13
### Stories Reporting Symptoms of Depression, Anxiety, and PTSD

|  | Depression (%) | Anxiety (%) | PTSD (%) |
|---|---|---|---|
| Two or more | 28 | 12 | 29 |
| Three or more | 8 | 3 | 8 |
| Four or more | 3 | 1 | 1 |

Two chi-square tests revealed that the number of depression, PTSD, and anxiety symptoms reported is positively linked to the number of different IIRAIRA-related effects reported. These results are expected in that longer texts should logically list a greater number of both effects and symptoms. The length of the texts was not measured; results therefore cannot be adjusted for any possible effects from such a variable. Table 14 illustrates the correlation between numbers of effects reported and symptoms of depression.

### Table 14
### Depression

|  | Dep ≤1 | Dep = 2 | Dep ≥ 3 | Sum |
|---|---|---|---|---|
| Total E < 2 | 28 | 6 | 0 | 34 |
| Total E = 2 | 28 | 7 | 0 | 35 |
| Total E = 3 | 29 | 9 | 1 | 38 |
| Total E > 3 | 25 | 9 | 11 | 45 |
| Sum | 110 | 30 | 12 | 152 |

*Note.* Degrees of freedom = 6; significance level = 0.05; critical value = 12.6; chi-square = 25.09.

$H_0$: Stories that report more effects do not describe more symptoms of depression.

$H_1$: Stories that report more effects describe more symptoms of depression.

Since the chi-square of 25.09 exceeded the critical value of 12.6, the null hypothesis was rejected. The conclusion was reached that stories reporting a higher number of different symptoms of depression also reported a higher number of different IIRAIRA-related effects. Therefore, by implication, it follows that stories reporting a lower number of depressive symptoms report lower IIRAIRA-related effects.

Table 15 illustrates the correlation between numbers of effects reported and symptoms of PTSD.

**Table 15**
**PTSD**

|  | PTSD ≤ 1 | PTSD = 2 | PTSD ≥ 3 | Sum |
|---|---|---|---|---|
| Total E < 2 | 29 | 4 | 1 | 34 |
| Total E = 2 | 30 | 3 | 2 | 35 |
| Total E = 3 | 31 | 5 | 2 | 38 |
| Total E > 3 | 18 | 20 | 7 | 45 |
| Sum | 108 | 32 | 12 | 152 |

*Note.* Degrees of freedom = 6; significance level = 0.05; critical value = 14.5; chi-square = 30.5.

$H_0$: Stories that report more effects do not describe more symptoms of PTSD.
$H_1$: Stories that report more effects describe more symptoms of PTSD.

With a chi-square of 30.5 exceeding the critical value of 14.5, the null hypothesis was rejected. The conclusion was reached that stories reporting a higher number of different symptoms of PTSD also reported a higher number of different IIRAIRA-related effects. By implication, it follows that those reporting a lower number of PTSD symptoms also report a lower number of IIRAIRA-related effects.

## *Examining the Controls: Effects*

Figure 6 illustrates, on a percentage basis, distribution of effects reported in the control data stories compared with those in the website self-reported stories.

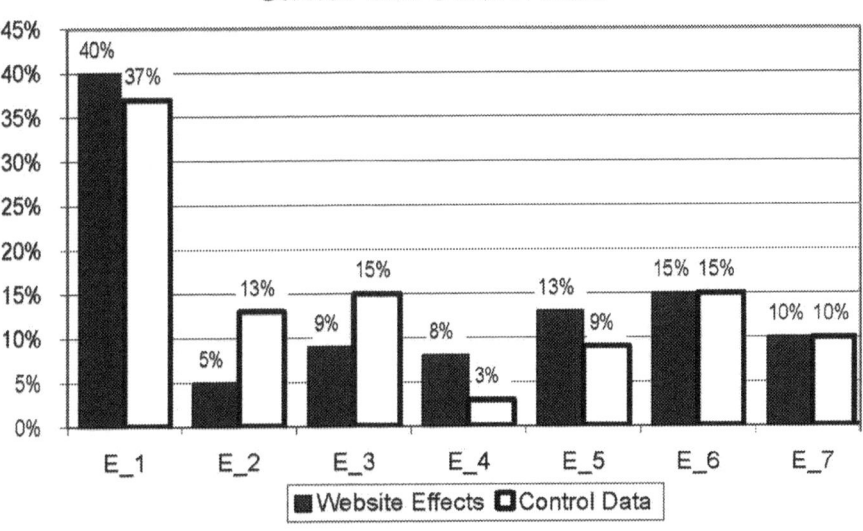

*Figure 6.* Distribution of website effects and control data effects.

The following test was used to compare effects reported on the website with those reported in the control data.

$H_0$: There is no difference between the reported website data effects and the control data effects.

$H_1$: There is a difference between the reported website data effects and the control data effects.

**Table 16**

*Comparison of Effects Reported on Website with Those Reported in Control Data*

| Observed | E_1 | E_2 | E_3 | E_4 | E_5 | E_6 | E_7 | Sum |
|---|---|---|---|---|---|---|---|---|
| Website data effects | 318 | 40 | 69 | 66 | 105 | 116 | 79 | 798 |
| Control data effects | 60 | 21 | 24 | 5 | 14 | 24 | 16 | 164 |
| Total | 378 | 61 | 93 | 71 | 119 | 140 | 95 | 957 |
| **Expected** | E_1 | E_2 | E_3 | E_4 | E_5 | E_6 | E_7 | Sum |
| Website data effects | 313 | 51 | 77 | 59 | 99 | 116 | 79 | 793 |
| Control data effects | 65 | 10 | 16 | 12 | 20 | 24 | 16 | 164 |
| Total | 378 | 61 | 93 | 71 | 119 | 140 | 95 | 962 |

*Note.* Degrees of freedom = 6; significance level = 0.05; critical value = 12.6; chi-square = 25.5.

Because the chi-square of 25.5 exceeded the critical value of 12.6 at the 5% level of significance, the null hypothesis was rejected, and a difference was found between the website data effects and the control data effects. For example, the journalists and community hearing speakers were far more likely than website authors to address the traumatic experience of arrest and loss of confidence in the legal system. Proportionally, the website self-reports were more likely to focus on the effect of cultural displacement than were the journalists, and the perception of injustice effect was more pronounced in the self-reports than in the journalistic accounts.

## *Examining the Controls: Symptoms*

Figure 7 illustrates, on a percentage basis, distribution of symptoms reported in the control data stories compared with those in the website self-reported stories.

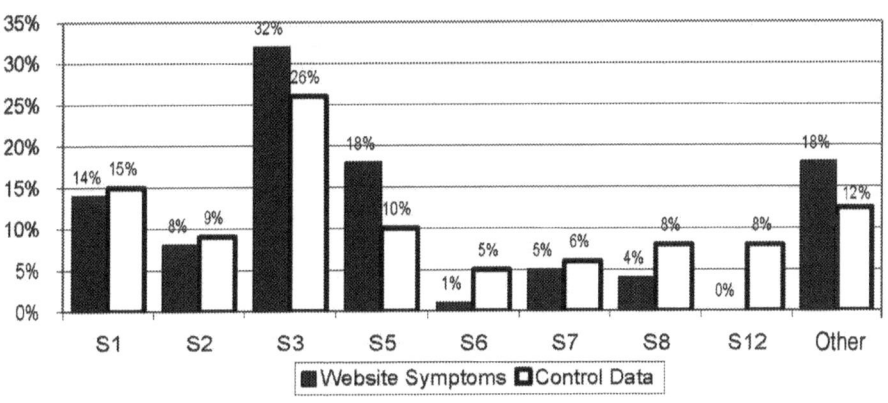

Figure 7. Distribution of website symptoms and control data symptoms.

A chi-square test was conducted comparing the self-reported website symptoms and those reported by journalists and at the community hearing. Symptoms that yielded expected frequencies at a level of fewer than five per symptom were grouped for testing purposes.

$H_0$: There is no difference between the reported website data symptoms and the control data symptoms.

$H_1$: There is a difference between the reported website data symptoms and the control data symptoms.

**Table 17**
*Comparison of Symptoms Reported on Website with Those Reported in Control Data*

| Observed | S1 | S2 | S3 | S5 | S6 | S7 | S8 | S12 | Other | Sum |
|---|---|---|---|---|---|---|---|---|---|---|
| Website data symptoms | 55 | 31 | 94 | 37 | 18 | 23 | 27 | 27 | 43 | 355 |
| Control data symptoms | 10 | 6 | 23 | 13 | 1 | 4 | 3 | 0 | 13 | 73 |
| Total | 65 | 37 | 117 | 50 | 19 | 27 | 30 | 27 | 56 | 428 |
| **Expected** | **S1** | **S2** | **S3** | **S5** | **S6** | **S7** | **S8** | **S12** | **Other** | **Sum** |
| Website data symptoms | 54 | 31 | 97 | 41 | 16 | 22 | 25 | 22 | 46 | 355 |
| Control data symptoms | 11 | 6 | 20 | 9 | 3 | 5 | 5 | 5 | 10 | 73 |
| Total | 65 | 37 | 117 | 50 | 19 | 27 | 30 | 27 | 56 | 428 |

*Note.* Degrees of freedom = 8; significance level = 0.05; critical value = 15.5; chi-square = 13.6. S4 is not included in Other.

As the chi-square of 13.6 did not exceed the critical value of 15.5, the null hypothesis could not be rejected. There was, therefore, no difference between the self-reported website symptoms and the symptoms reported in the control data.

# 5

## *Discussion*

## SUMMARY

IIRAIRA has a psychological impact not only on legal permanent U.S. residents but also on their families. The purpose for which the law was enacted, the manner in which it is executed, the disallowance of extenuating legal circumstances, all predictably guarantee a tragic outcome.

The study found that 96% of website authors reported a tragic effect on their lives and 70% reported symptoms of emotional distress that are indications of depression and PTSD. On average, each story reported 5.2 effects and 2.3 symptoms. Seventy-seven percent of the authors experienced the effect of perception of injustice described as cognitive shock. Family separation, cultural displacement, and economic losses were three of the effects caused by IIRAIRA. The most prevalent symptoms experienced as a result of the law were hopelessness/despair, sadness, shock and fear.

Two moderately significant relationships were found. One was that arrest leads to shock and the second is that family separation leads to sadness. This demonstrates that the manner in which IIRAIRA is executed causes the experience of shock. The second finding shows that the provisions of the law cause families to be separated and experience sadness as a result.

Another study finding is that writers who perceived IIRAIRA as unjust reported more symptoms, which can be interpreted either that the perception of injustice intensifies the emotional effect, or that the emotional effect intensifies the perception of injustice.

Text examples that illustrate the perception of injustice reflect the cognitive shock that throws into confusion the writers' concept of what the U.S. stands for. Some authors describe the law as Hitlerian, un-American, an example of Nazism. They point out that it strikes down the judicial branch of government and violates the constitution, while destroying family integrity and betraying its own

71

U.S.-born children. They question IIRAIRA's purpose, its unfairness, its inherent injustice, and the discriminatory actions flowing from it. If not addressed, the combination of this cognitive shock and the many effects caused by IIRAIRA portends a future of serious psychological distress for those subject to the law.

Demonstrating how IIRAIRA has a domino effect on the whole family, the research finds that there is no significant difference between the type of symptoms reported by detainees and those reported by families of detainees.

In 3% of website stories, those affected by IIRAIRA reported four or more symptoms of depression; 8% reported three or more symptoms of depression; 8% reported three or more symptoms of PTSD. Two or more symptoms of depression were reported in 28% of the stories, and 29% reported two or more symptoms of PTSD. These findings reveal that symptoms of depression and PTSD are positively linked to IIRAIRA-related effects. Anxiety symptoms were also present but to a lower extent.

The last study analysis comparing the website stories to the control data shows that symptoms are consistent in both groups. The effects distribution is not consistent between both groups, but all effects were present in both groups. These findings demonstrate that the website stories are valid and that IIRAIRA causes effects and symptoms.

Specific diagnoses are impossible without directed questioning, non-verbal clues provided by the interviewee and/or family members, and the opportunity to follow the lead of the individual being interviewed. Relative to anxiety and PTSD, where significant physical manifestations are part of the diagnostic criteria, an open-ended, web-based text description is unlikely to provide the level of detailed information required for a diagnosis.

Regardless, the consistently strong manifestations of hopelessness/despair, helplessness and sadness lead the researcher to believe there are strong indications of depression in this sample of individuals. Additionally, the indirect signs of anxiety and PTSD are present, but not strong enough to use with certainty. The literature suggests that those who experience family separation and cultural displacement typically experience symptomology consistent with those experiences. The sample data repeatedly cite such experiences, so it is not unreasonable to expect that these symptoms are present, but not reported.

# CORRELATIONS BETWEEN STUDY FINDINGS AND REVIEWED LITERATURE

The tone of the literature related to IIRAIRA and its unjust effects on families can be illustrated by a quote from the *Harvard Law Review*:

> It is time to recognize that deportation of legal permanent residents for criminal and other post-entry conduct is punishment. If it must be done, then it must be done with specific, substantive constitutional protections. It should, at the very least, not be done retroactively, without counsel, or without a right to bail. If we must deport long-term residents as a dubious means of social control, let us at least strive to call things as they are. (Kanstroom, 2000, p.1935)

Like the scholars and legal experts who perceive IIRAIRA as unjust, those who have suffered from the law are strong in their expressed beliefs that it is "unconstitutional," "unfair" and "not right." Each narrative in the study, no matter the source, followed a similar pattern. Extracts from the control data corresponded closely to those of the website stories: first the facts were stated; then concerns were expressed regarding family separation and cultural displacement as a result of obvious injustice, particularly as it relates to violations of the norms of due process.

The authors of the website self-reports and the control data narratives agree that IIRAIRA is unjust in both theory and practice. They cite retroactivity, double jeopardy, lack of judicial review, and the potential of life sentences for minor offenses. The frequency with which perception of injustice was mentioned is the strongest and most consistent trend in the study results.

Perceived injustice intensifies psychological and social trauma. Those who are subject to procedural inconsistencies that operate against their interests are particularly prone to perceiving a situation as unjust. This research confirms that IIRAIRA detainees and their families perceive the law to be unjust. The perception of injustice heightens the suffering of those affected by IIRAIRA.

From the literature, we can see that this perception is not without foundation. There seems to be historical continuity in using immigrants, and fear of immigrants, as scapegoats for this country's problems. It is an American pattern. Family separation and cultural displacement have been a consequence of national policy for a long time, especially relative to those who are not citizens and are therefore sometimes considered to be outside the protection of the law. While the study participants did not express much awareness of the historical background of IIRAIRA, often declaring that such a thing could not or should not happen in America, the harshness of the treatment dealt to those who are affected by this law is consistent with documented precedent.

According to the reviewed literature and the study data analyses, the anticipated effects of IIRAIRA have actually taken place. The literature suggests that those who are unjustly treated experience anger, frustration, and, finally, helplessness. This is what is seen in the data extracted from this study. The literature predicts that individuals confronted with such injustice will experience negative feelings, symptomology of depression, perhaps anxiety and/or PTSD. The data bear this out: the most frequently reported symptomology is that associated with depression (hopelessness/despair), and there are indicators of the other related problems. The perception of IIRAIRA is consistent in archival review, journalistic accounts, and the stated experiences of the detainees and their families.

As noted in the literature review, those subjected to injustice, as well as those who perceive themselves to be, see their natural responses of anger and frustration devolve into a sense of helplessness and despair that is accompanied by a heightened fear of potential threat. While the study data do not show the expected levels of anger and frustration, anger is apparent, especially in the overall tone of the writings and in the expressions of perceptions of injustice. Importantly, the data suggest that a significant number of the victims of IIRAIRA have already progressed to a state of despair stemming from hopelessness/helplessness.

Alternatively, one could read the stories and find an overall theme of anger without identifying a single phrase that explicitly uses the word. So in this study, anger could have been under-reported solely due to the method of codification. On the other hand, every expression of perceived injustice could have been coded as also containing anger, and the findings would conform to the predictions in the literature review, which is that frustration and aggression result from experiencing an unfair situation with unfavorable consequences (Krehbeil & Cropanzano, 2000).

Research has shown that family separation, economic loss, and cultural displacement can cause negative effects such as behavior problems, lower academic performance, depression, alcohol/narcotics abuse, suicide, violence, fear, loss of confidence, and despair (Beiser et al., 1995; Essau & Petermann, 1999; Long, 2003; Rumberger & Larson, 1998; Scanlon & Devine 2001; Tucker et al., 1998). The findings in this research confirm that IIRAIRA causes family separation, economic loss, and cultural displacement. While not intended to diagnose, the study revealed strong indications of symptomology that should be followed up on, to confirm the type of psychological effects suffered by people who experience the negative effects of IIRAIRA.

Indications of the symptomology expressed in the data suggest a link between IIRAIRA and a number of psychological and social problems. Family members report experiencing the same type of symptomology as those who are/have been detained and deported. Both groups reported the same types of symptoms, in the same proportions: strong indications of depression and signs of anxiety and PTSD. There are even documented cases of suicide as a result of this law. In such extreme cases, general conclusions about the depth of the problem within the legal permanent resident community can be arrived at. Individuals and family members who have been affected by IIRAIRA suffer visible harm as surely as if they had been exposed to the shock of a caustic chemical.

# MATCHING STUDY CONCLUSIONS WITH LITERATURE REVIEW

Just over half the reports in the website sample contain explicit textual descriptions of symptomology related to depression, anxiety or PTSD. The consistently solid results suggesting helplessness, sadness and hopelessness/despair indicate there are strong indications of depression in this sample of individuals. Indirect signs of anxiety and PTSD are present but are not strong enough to lead to solid conclusions. The literature suggests that those who undergo family separation and cultural displacement similar to what is suffered under IIRAIRA typically exhibit symptomology compatible with the negative effects of those events. The study sample consistently cites such experiences, so it is reasonable to expect that these symptoms are present even when not reported.

Those who expressed symptomology related to the experience of IIRAIRA reported higher levels of perception of injustice. Of the 87 cases of reported symptoms, 70 mentioned perceptions of injustice one or more times. Of the 66 cases without reported symptoms, only 42 mentioned perceptions of injustice one or more times. Therefore, the researcher finds that there is a difference in perception of injustice between the individuals who reported symptoms and those who did not. This result conforms with the literature that predicts a relationship between the perception of injustice and the severity or intensity of the emotional effects of that injustice. Although this result is not statistically valid, as the sample is not random, its conformity with the literature suggests the predicted relationship is credible.

# EXAMINING THE CONTROLS

Comparing the website self-reports with the control data provided confirmation of the study results. The control data were independent of the self-reports, and included additional person-to-person interview interaction which elicited greater detail and confirmed the underlying facts of the website IIRAIRA-related experiences.

The symptoms reported in the control data were consistent with the self-reported symptomology in the website stories. But distribution of the effects reported in the control data was not consistent with that in the self-reports. A comparison of the effects reported in the control data to those described in the website self-reports showed that the journalists were far more likely to report the traumatic experience of arrest and loss of confidence in the legal system, while proportionately, the self-reports were more likely to focus on the effects of cultural displacement and the perception of injustice.

There are several possible reasons for these differences. In a journalistic report, the effects of IIRAIRA are usually mentioned only once, in a general overview. Because editing constraints limit the repetition of those effects when individual IIRAIRA-related stories are recounted further on in the article, symptoms that recur often in real life and are therefore mentioned frequently in the website stories are either not cited at all by journalists, or are mentioned only once. Additionally, because of dissimilarities in focus and background, it is likely that the perceptions of a third party, such as a journalist, would differ from those of the reporting individuals. Therefore, since several edited cases may have been extracted from a single journalistic account, the study ratio was skewed because of this format/perception anomaly.

Whether they were being interviewed, testifying at a community hearing or telling their story on the website, all IIRAIRA-affected families reported suffering the same types of negative effects. But because study information retrieved from the control data had already been edited, those accounts contained significantly fewer repetitions of symptoms. However, data analyses indicated that despite diverse reporting methods, the trends remained the same, a finding that validates the research.

# POSSIBLE RATIONALES FOR UNSUPPORTED HYPOTHESES AND UNEXPECTED RESULTS

The primary unexpected result of this study is that the data did not show higher levels of anger and more signs of PTSD. As discussed earlier in this chapter, the codification method used may explain these results. Because the researcher chose to be rather conservative with the text extracts, only those reporting anger explicitly were codified as such. If a looser standard were adopted, allowing expressions of perceived injustice to be cross-coded as expressions of anger, it is possible the expected levels may have been met and even exceeded.

Similarly, it appeared reasonable to predict that high levels of PTSD symptomology would be described in the stories of IIRAIRA-affected detainees and their families, since the prerequisites for PTSD are built into most IIRAIRA-related experiences: (a) a traumatic and unexpected arrest is experienced directly by the detainee and often witnessed by the family; (b) the arrest and subsequent detention threatens to destroy the detainee's life and cause the individual or family members to experience intense fear, helplessness, and/or horror.

But the data showed no confirmation of the stages of PTSD. There were no reports of re-experiencing the traumatic event; there were no strong reports of avoidance of stimuli associated with the trauma, or numbing of general responsiveness; there were a few reports of sleep disturbances, but the other signs of persistent increased arousal were not reported in the texts.

Does this mean that none of the individuals who have suffered the effects of IIRAIRA have PTSD? It probably does not. It may be that the self-selected sample of individuals who tell their stories do not include those whose functioning has been more severely affected. It could also be that without specific probing, such information is unlikely to be volunteered in a public forum such as the Internet. Still, the data suggested that IIRAIRA is not causing obvious or widespread cases of PTSD. As noted in the literature, perhaps certain individuals with a predisposition to PTSD are experiencing these symptoms but have not reported them publicly. Or it may be that IIRAIRA-related trauma produces other psychological symptoms than PTSD.

# CLINICAL IMPLICATIONS

The most direct way to change a perception of injustice is to remove the perceived injustice. In the case of IIRAIRA, Congressman Bob Filner (D-CA) has introduced a bill (HR3272) that will redress some of the grievances of legal permanent U.S. residents. Passage of HR3272 could pave the way for family reunification and possible compensation for those affected by the law. While the legislative process continues, mental health professionals continue to interact with individuals and families who remain under constant threat of deportation. Until the law is repealed or other remedial measures are taken, the therapist or social worker who treats affected families must be aware of IIRAIRA and its implications, and take steps during assessment to ensure that each patient is appropriately treated while being properly protected.

IIRAIRA appears to have been written to divide, punish, and exclude in order to control, so its language is sufficiently inclusive to affect the entire legal resident community. Minor offenses such as hair-pulling have been reclassified as aggravated felonies, offenses already satisfied through time served or acquittal/dismissal have been re-charged and re-punished, and retroactive sentences for these satisfied offenses have been increased to conform to aggravated felony status.

Through a complicated set of conditions and regulations, hundreds of thousands of individuals and their families have been rendered instantly deportable and denied legal recourse. Struggling to resolve their situation, those without financial resources are often helpless to defend themselves, and those who had funds have found them quickly depleted to the point that they have lost homes, businesses, retirement funds and college savings.

Amazingly, a segment of the legal resident community is still either ignorant of IIRAIRA's consequences or in denial about the jeopardy into which it puts them. "It will never happen to us" is said to avoid facing the reality of the law's scope. Thus, when some legal residents are seized and deported at the time they apply to the INS for citizenship, or apprehended and put into detention as they come through an airport on their return from a trip, they are stunned.

From a clinical perspective, the therapist must understand that IIRAIRA treats legal permanent U.S. residents differently from naturalized citizens or those who are native-born. Specifically, the therapist must inform a legal permanent U.S. resident patient, or anyone who reports on the behavior of a resident, that prior minor offenses may now be dealt with as aggravated felonies, which are deportable offenses. Unless the patient clearly understands the possible IIRAIRA-related effects of revealing sensitive personal information which by law must be reported to the authorities, he/she could inadvertently set life-changing events in motion, and the therapist involved could unintentionally harm a family rather than heal it.

At the present time, few people outside the immigration law community are aware of IIRAIRA. To rectify this situation, development courses for mental health professionals should include a brief overview of the law and its implications, as well as assessment information particular to IIRAIRA-affected patients. The law has created ethical problems for all health professionals. For the sake of both patients and therapists, the ways in which these problems affect treatment must be clearly understood and thoroughly discussed, nationwide, during professional development sessions.

A particular effect of the law that should be recognized in assessments and treatments is the perception of injustice common to IIRAIRA-affected patients. The issues of personal/geographical separation, economic loss and cultural displacement being faced by the families are aggravated by the perception of injustice. Health professionals who do not recognize this can disbelieve a patient who presents with such issues, adding to his/her trauma. It is critical that the therapist validate this perception, evidenced in symptoms of depression, anxiety, and PTSD, and that both patient and family are helped to develop long-term coping strategies. Additionally, patient assessments should reflect that IIRAIRA has turned the legal permanent resident community into a destabilized population frequently on the move. The therapist can help by establishing early on how much time is available for any treatment, and by planning accordingly.

A therapist does not treat any patients, including those affected by IIRAIRA, in a vacuum. Since the families' mental health status is likely to remain poor so long as this law exists, the therapist can provide information and support that will enable clients to cope. Ideally, groups can be set up to pass along information, educate clients and the public about the legal situation, and perhaps devote time and effort to the political processes that can change the law. Sometimes an effective treatment for depression is to help someone else. If IIRAIRA-affected families' energies can be directed toward changing the law and helping other families in need, they may regain the sense of hope and power that is currently missing from their lives.

Where IIRAIRA intersects with therapy, attorneys and therapists must be informed and maintain contact with one another. It can be mutually beneficial for members of the legal community to liaison with members of the therapeutic community. Legal professionals could establish a working relationship with therapists who are aware of the unique circumstances facing their clients, and would become a resource for therapists whose work may depend on knowledge of this law when providing therapy to legal permanent U.S. residents and their families.

The therapeutic community has unwittingly been thrust to the forefront of the immigration debate. A therapist has a legal obligation to report certain behaviors, such as child abuse, elder abuse and domestic violence. Since the passage of IIRAIRA, when the abuser is a legal permanent U.S. resident, the therapist's report could lead to more than an ordinary law enforcement intervention. Under IIRAIRA, child abuse, elder abuse and domestic violence have been reclassified as deportable offenses, so the therapist's action could potentially lead to additional trauma for the patient's family, with one parent deported and the other left alone to fend for the children. In situations like this, therapists must ask themselves where the greater good can be found. Many mental health professionals who have not yet faced a situation like this are currently unaware that they risk being caught in an ethical dilemma because of IIRAIRA. The consent and release of information forms currently used by the therapeutic community in the United States should be amended to include information regarding the consequences of IIRAIRA. Without waiting for that change to be effected, therapists should disclose to their clients the consequences of IIRAIRA and its effects on legal permanent residents and their families so the clients are aware of any additional risks they may face in disclosing reportable information.

The immigrant community, a subset of which is the legal resident population, has a complex social and family dynamic. Its members will either adopt or reject certain values/norms from the majority population, or they will remain conflicted about them, undecided as to whether they wish to add them to the ones they bring with them when they immigrate. The values/norms that children of immigrants adopt from the majority population are often different from those adhered to by their parents. If mental health professionals are to serve immigrant clients well, they must meet the challenge of understanding not only the basics of human development, but also the complexities of their clients' social/family structure and historical/political background.

Because the majority population influences new residents' experiences by either welcoming or rejecting them, governmental leaders promote a society's unfavorable perception of immigrants when they enact laws motivated more by political pressure than by justice. IIRAIRA is a law with very drastic negative consequences for the legal permanent resident community. The horrors resulting from IIRAIRA demonstrate the consequences of passing punitive legislation, either knowingly or without sufficient awareness of what is being enacted. Certain offenses have always been deemed deportable by the legal system. By greatly expanding the categories of what is now deportable, and by imposing punishments out of all proportion to any crime committed, IIRAIRA becomes the most recent challenge to the skills of mental health professionals and the most recent example of immigration legislation to be viewed as unworthy of a society that calls itself humane.

# RESEARCH IMPLICATIONS AND METHODOLOGY IMPROVEMENTS

The primary weakness of the constant comparison method is inconsistency in the codification of text extracts. Simply put, when drawing from authors with different educational backgrounds and widely varying levels of literacy and vocabulary, it is difficult to codify the text information in a consistent manner.

To improve this situation, a team approach may be useful. While extracting text and codifying it, several judgements must be made. Is this valid? Is it consistent for the standards (key words) devised for this code? Is it consistent with the other text extracts already coded in this manner? If these questions are answered incorrectly, information will be put in the wrong place. With only one set of eyes reviewing the coding for consistency, mistakes are possible. A team approach could reduce the potential for such mistakes. Ideally, team members look at the information sequentially, examining the data set for inconsistencies. One person may label a text extract as "fear," while another may label it as "worry." This creates a healthy debate over the key words and other standards used to extract the data, and can help determine the final designation.

When examining extracts that have already been coded, the team of researchers could individually and as a group review the information to ensure that the extracts within a single code are similar enough to each other to provide consistency. This should lead to more reliable results when using the constant comparison method.

# SUGGESTIONS FOR FUTURE RESEARCH

This study, while important and interesting, is a first step, an approximation of the psychological and social damage caused by IIRAIRA. Further studies will require rigor beyond the scope of this dissertation, which serves to point the way forward.

There is an urgent need for a follow-up study with a personal interview component, to delve more deeply into the psychological and social effects of IIRAIRA. As long as the law remains unchanged, there is a great need to monitor and research the consequences for families and detainees who are being affected. A more detailed large-scale study may provide stronger proof that IIRAIRA is directly responsible for depression, anxiety and PTSD; such proof is precluded by the limited nature of this study.

Interdisciplinary teams of sociologists, political scientists, economists, and psychologists should study this law and its many consequences. Without an integrated approach, there is danger of focusing on single aspects of IIRAIRA instead of the wide range of its repercussions. Economists can investigate the law's unintended effect of forcing families onto government assistance. Political scientists can analyze members of Congress' perception of the law, and their motivations for passing it. Psychologists and sociologists can examine this and similar laws before they are passed, and educate lawmakers in regard to the negative consequences of their actions.

There should also be a study that gathers information to assess the repercussions of IIRAIRA. Has this law made our society more secure? Has the country been saved from violent criminals, who, by being deported, are no longer a threat to us? Are there families whose lives have been improved because one parent is permanently removed to another country? Such a study would be a useful control for the data found by means of other approaches.

Since the primary harm caused by IIRAIRA is family separation and cultural displacement, do those displaced individuals who have thoroughly assimilated into American culture suffer more, when deported, than those who are not yet acculturated? It seems reasonable that IIRAIRA-related perceptions of justice and injustice are closely tied to acculturation levels. Because the United States claims adherence to a higher standard of justice, is IIRAIRA-created cognitive dissonance greater for those who truly believe in America's values and ideals than it is for those who have not yet fully internalized these principles? A study that measures this difference could be valuable. Additionally, an investigation to determine if IIRAIRA causes more harm to deportees and families who are better off financially than to those who are not could reveal whether this law is more harsh toward those with greater or lesser economic power.

A study comparing this law with other countries' criminal exclusion policies would be useful for judging IIRAIRA's appropriateness. How do other countries deal with similar cases? Is there a cultural, political or geographical pattern? Should the U.S. consider using approaches adopted by others?

Lacking reliable figures, it is difficult to measure the magnitude of the law's overall effects. How many children have seen a parent deported under IIRAIRA? How many people, in total, have been affected by IIRAIRA? So far, there is no comprehensive number for IIRAIRA-related expulsions, though it appears to be in the tens of thousands every year. In 2001 alone, according to the Office of Immigration Statistics, over 70,000 were removed from the U.S. because of IIRAIRA (U.S. Citizenship and Immigration Services, 2002). This implies that hundreds of thousands of children and spouses are likely to be undergoing significant trauma because of those removals and the circumstances surrounding them. But we do not yet know the true numbers.

Additionally, while anecdotal evidence and historical patterns suggest that more men than women are expelled under IIRAIRA, the repercussions of separating fathers from their children are serious enough, but it is equally important to know how many mothers have been separated from their children under this law. Is the law applied differently when it comes to female deportees? This is information that should be gathered and studied.

It is critical to identify and track those affected by the law, particularly children who are exposed to traumatic, life-altering events. Unless these individuals are followed, those who can help may be losing a chance to intervene at a time when it will make a difference. Are dysfunctional and broken families being created by governmental actions? Has a whole new class of criminals been created?

When deportation forcibly separates people from their families and homes, it is predictable that some will return illegally. Those who are reapprehended could be sentenced to decades in prison. How much is this costing our society?

To determine the scope of IIRAIRA's negative effects, it is necessary to maintain contact with the individuals and families who are banished to the deportees' country of origin. Are they simply let loose to wander? Do they suffer beatings, additional imprisonment or other official punishment? How many stay in the country to which they are deported? How many try to return to the U.S.? How many U.S.-born children of deportees find themselves, because of IIRAIRA-related circumstances, in what is to them a foreign country?

As a practical matter, members of a society must know if the laws they enact promote justice or injustice. If deportation is truly a death sentence, as several website authors indicate, then the public should know this, and so should lawmakers who are responsible for such legislation. Without a study following the individuals who are sent away, the totality of IIRAIRA's effects cannot be known.

This seminal study has a significance beyond its limited scope. Punitive legislation like IIRAIRA follows a historical pattern of targeting a vulnerable segment of the U.S. population. Documenting IIRAIRA-related psychological and social consequences demonstrates that the ripple effect of traumatic negative life changes imposed by legislation creates depressed single parents, psychologically impaired children and disoriented deportees, all of which significantly impacts society. When the language of a law artificially creates felons, the victims of that law are labeled and treated as culprits. The consequences of IIRAIRA are created by the actions of those who legislated the law into existence and those who carry out its mandates, not by the actions of those who are its targets. This research serves as a reminder that psychological damage inevitably follows life-altering trauma, that suspending the legal protections of some makes us all equally vulnerable, and that only by examining the consequences of such legislative actions can we calculate the true costs of a law like IIRAIRA.

> "When will justice come to Athens?" they asked Thucydides.
> "Justice will not come to Athens until those who are not injured
> are as indignant as those who are."
>
> —Anonymous

# References

Amaral Dias, C. A., Vicente, T. N., Cabrita, M. F., & de Mendon, A. R. (1981). Transplantation, identity and drug addiction. *Bulletin of Narcotics, 33,* 21-26.

Amato, P. R. (1993). Children's adjustment to divorce: Theories, hypotheses and empirical support. *Journal of Marriage and the Family, 55,* 23-38.

American Psychiatric Association. (2000). *Diagnostic and statistical manual of mental disorders* (text revision). Washington, DC: Author.

Anderson, P. S. (1999, April 9). Immigration reform unfairly includes petty offenses. *The Herald*, p. 19A.

Balderrama, F. E., & Rodriguez, R. (2002). *Decade of betrayal: Mexican repatriation in the 1930s.* Albuquerque: University of New Mexico Press.

Beiser, M., Dion, R., Gotowiec, A., Hyman, I., & Vu, N. (1995). Immigrant and refugee children in Canada. *Canadian Journal of Psychiatry, 40,* 67-72.

Bender, M. (1996). *Bender's Immigration and Nationality Act.* New York: Matthew Bender & Co.

Boman, B., & Edwards, M. (1984). The Indochinese refugee: An overview. *Australian and New Zealand Journal of Psychiatry, 18,* 40-52.

Butcher, K. F., & Piehl, A. M. (1999, February). *The role of deportation in the incarceration of immigrants* (National Bureau of Economic Research Working Paper No. w6974). Retrieved October 24, 2003, from http://www.nber.org/papers/w6974.

Chu, H. M. (1972). Migration and mental disorder in Taiwan. In W. Lebra (Ed.), *Transcultural research in mental health* (pp. 295-325). Honolulu: East West Center Press.

Colon, Y. (1999, February 18). Texas congressman's clout on immigration reso-
nates: Smith scuttles INS' plan to free criminals. *Miami Herald*, p. B1, col.
2.

Dube, K. C. (1968). Mental disorder in Agra. *Social Psychiatry, 3,* 139-143.

Ekblad, S. (1993). Psychosocial adaptation of chidren while housed in a Swedish
refugee camp: Aftermath of the collapse of Yugoslavia. *Stress Medicine, 9,*
159-166.

Esau, C. A., & Petermann, F. (1999). *Depressive disorders in children and adolescents: Epidemiology, risk factors and treatment.* Northvale, NJ: Jason Aron-
son.

Espenshade, T. J., Baraka, J. L., & Huber, G. A. (1997). Implications of the
1996 Welfare and Immigration Reform Acts for US. *Population and Development Review, 23*(4), 769-801.

Farias, P. J. (1991). Emotional distress and its sociopolitical correlates in Salva-
doran refugees: Analysis of a clinical sample. *Culture, Medicine and Psychiatry, 15,* 167-192.

Flores, E., & Duran, L. (1998). Immigration raids shatter families and human
rights. *The Progressive.* Retrieved November 2003 from http://www.
progressive.org/mpflores1198.htm

Fragomen, A. T., Jr. (1997). The Illegal Immigration Reform and Immigrant
Responsibility Act of 1996: An overview. *International Migration Review,
31*(2), 438-460.

Harris, T. (2001). Recent development in understanding the psychosocial aspects
of depression. *British Medical Bulletin, 57,* 17-32.

Huffman, K., Vernoy, M., & Vernoy, J. (1997). *Psychology in action* (4th ed.).
New York: John Wiley.

Hughes, R., Jr. (1996). *Report: The effects of divorce on children,* Department of
Family Relations and Human Development, Internet In-service on Children and Divorce, Ohio State University. Retrieved December 2, 2003,
from http://www.hec.ohiostate.edu/famlife/divorce/effects.htm

Ippolito, M., & Badie, R. (2001, February 2). Immigrant shoplifter's case could be landmark. *Atlanta Journal-Constitution*, p. C7.

Jackson, S., Feder, L., Forde, D. R., Davis, R. C., Maxwell, C. D., & Taylor, B. G. (2003, June). *Batterer intervention programs: Where do we go from here?* (Special Report NCJ 195079). Retrieved November 29, 2003, from http://www.ojp.usdoj.gov/nij/vawprog/pubs.html

Jones, G. (2003, July 15). Apology sought for Latino "repatriation" drive in '30s. *Los Angeles Times*, p. B1.

Jordan, B. (1995, February 24). Testimony to House Immigration Subcommittee. Retrieved September 24, 2003, from http://www.fairus.org/Research/Research.cfm?ID=2306&c=111&insearch=barbara%20and%20jordan%20and%201995%20and%20house%20and%20immigration%20and%20subcommittee%20 and %20testimony.

Kanstroom, D. (2000). Deportation, social control, and punishment: Some thoughts about why hard laws make bad cases. *Harvard Law Review, 118,* 1890-1935.

*Keeping our communities safe is INS' top priority.* (2000, April 18). Retrieved June 21, 2003, from http://www.uscis.gov/graphics/publicaffairs/statements/article/htm

Kessler, R. C., Mickelson, K. D., & Williams, D. R. (1999). The prevalence, distribution, and meantal health correlates of perceived discrimination in the United States. *Journal of Health and Social Behavior, 40,* 208-230.

Kim, U. (1988). *Acculturation of Korean immigrants to Canada.* Unpublished doctoral dissertation, Queen's University, Kingston, Canada.

Kraaij, V., Kremers, I., Arrensman, E., & Kerkhof, A. (1998). *Life events over the life cycle and depression in late life: Suicide prevention: The global context.* New York: Plenum Press.

Krehbeil, P. J., & Cropanzano, R. (2000). Procedural justice, outcome favorability, and emotion. *Social Justice Research, 13*(4), 339-360.

Lewis, A. (2000, January 8). Long-term LPR faces deportation for hair-pulling. *New York Times*, p. A13, col. 1.

Lipman, E. (2002). Child well-being in single-mother families. *Family and Society, 41,* 75-82.

Long, O. D. (2003). Swedish study indicates single parenting has a significant adverse impact on children. *Lancet.* Retrieved December 2, 2003, from http://news.fairfaxbar.org/printarticle.asp?article=412andarchive=true

Mace, G., & Roane, M. M. (2001). Bills would relax terms of deportation laws. *Akron Beacon-Journal,* p. B8.

Macpherson, M. (1992-1993). *Working through the trauma of political oppression: Focus on Eastern Europe and the USSR.* Berlin: Integral Studies, FRG.

Magagnini, S. (2003, July 16). 1 million of Mexican descent paid heavy price. *Sacramento Bee,* p. 1A. Retrieved July 18, 2003, from http://www.sacbee.com/content/lifestyle/history/story/7041676p-7989982c.html

Majodina, Z. (1989). Exile as a chronic stressor. *International Journal of Mental Health, 18,* 87-94.

Martinez, R. (n.d.). *The border and human rights.* Unpublished manuscript, American Friends Service Committee.

Maxwell, B. (1998, November 29). Deporting a parent. *St. Petersburg Times,* p. 1D. Retrieved January 13, 1999, from http://pqasb.pqarchiver.com/sptimes/index.html?ts=1077562699 (click on "Other Archives").

Mayada, N. S. (1983). Psychosocial welfare of refugees: An expanding service area of social work. *International Social Work, 26,* 47-55.

Maykut, P., & Morehouse, R. (1994). *Beginning qualitative research: A philosophic and practical guide.* London: Falmer Press.

McBride, M. J. (1999). Migrants and asylum seekers: Policy responses in the United States to immigrants and refugees from Central America and the Caribbean. *International Migration, 37*(1), 289-317.

McDonnell, P. J. (1998a, March 14). The Mosquera family. *Los Angeles Times,* p. B1.

McDonnell, P. J. (1998b, March 14). Tragedy: Teenager kills himself after his father (a legal resident for 29 years) is sent to Colombia because of a $10 marijuana sale in 1989. *Los Angeles Times*, p. B1.

Melton, G. B., & Barry, F. D. (1994). *Protecting children from abuse and neglect: Foundations for a new national strategy.* New York: Guilford Press.

*Mental health: Culture, race, ethnicity.* (2001). Chapter 2: Racism and mental health. US Surgeon General's Report. US Department of Health and Human Services, Office of the Surgeon General, SAMHSA. Retrieved November 2, 2003, from http://www.mentalhealth.org/cre/ch2_racism_discrimination_andmental_health.asp

*Mental health: A report of the Surgeon General.* (1999). Chapter 4: Stressful life events. Retrieved November 1, 2003, from http://www.surgeongeneral.gov/library/mentalhealth/chapter4/sec1.html

Miller, R. L. (1999). *West's American government* (2d ed.). Cincinnati, OH: West Educational Publishers.

Miron, R. (2003a, October 1). Despair of Palestinian children. *BBC News.* Retrieved November 12, 2003, from http:/www.palestinemonitor.org/Feature/despair_or_pal_children.htm

Miron, R. (2003b, September 30). Israel's suffering children. *BBC News.* Retrieved November 12, 2003, from http://news.bbc.co.uk/2hi/middle_east/3152428.stm

Mollica, R. F. (1990). Refugee trauma: The impact of public policy on adaptation and disability. In W. H. Holtzman & T. H. Bornemann (Eds.), *Mental health of immigrants and refugees* (pp. 251-260). Austin: University of Texas.

Morawitz, N. (1998). Rethinking retroactive deportation laws and the due process clause. *New York University Law Review, 73*(1), 97-161.

Morgan, M. C., Wingard, D. L., & Felice, M. E. (1984). Subcultural differences in alcohol use among youth. *Journal of Adolescent Health Care, 5,*191-195.

Nagata, D. K. (1993). *Legacy of injustice: Exploring the cross-generational impact of the Japanese American internment (critical issues in social justice).* New York: Kluwer Academic/Plenum Press.

National Institute of Mental Health. (1999, September/Updated October 5, 2001). *Facts about post-traumatic stress disorder* (Publication No. OM-99 4157 Revised). Retrieved September 21, 2003, from http://www.nimh.nih.gov/anxiety/ptsdfacts.cfm

Nicasso, P. M., & Pate, J. K. (1984). Analysis of problems of resettlement of the Indochinese refugees in the United States. *Social Psychiatry, 19,* 135-141.

Office of Justice Programs. (2003). Family violence research and statistics. Retrieved November 29, 2003, from http://www.ojp:usdoj.gov/familyviolence/publications.

Piscova, M. (1992). The family in a situation of social dependence; Ridona v. situacii socialnej odkazanosti. Kontexty a suvislosti. *Socilogia, 24*(6), 515-526. Retrieved June 1, 2003, from http://www.warwick.ac.uk/fac/soc/complabstuds/russia/references.doc

Prakash, A. P. (1997). Changing the rules: Arguing against retroactive application of deportation statutes. *New York University Law Review, 72*(6), 1420-1461.

Ren, X. S., Amick, B., & Williams, D. R. (1999). Racial/ethnic disparities in health: The interplay between discrimination and socioeconomic status. *Ethnicity and Disease, 9,* 151-165.

Rumberger, R. W., & Larson, K. A. (1998). Student mobility and the increased risk of high school dropout. *American Journal of Education, 107,* 1-35.

Sack, W. H. (1985). Posttraumatic stress disorders in children. *Integrative Psychiatry, 3,* 162-164.

Sagi-Schwartz, A. (2003). Long-term traumatic stress in Holocaust survivors. *American Journal of Psychiatry, 160,* 1086-1092.

San, L. A. (2003, June 10). Suben deportaciones. *El Mexicano,* p. 4.

Scanlon, E., & Devine, K. (2001). Residential mobility and youth well-being: Research, policy, and practice. *Journal of Sociology and Social Welfare, 28*(1), 119-136.

Schneller, D. P. (1976). *The prisoner's family: A study of the effects of imprisonment on the families of prisoners.* San Francisco: R&E Research Associates.

Shaw, R. (1987). *Children of imprisoned fathers.* London: Hodder and Stoughton.

Silver, R. C., Holman, E. A., & McIntosh, D. M. (2002). Nationwide longitudinal study of psychological responses to September 11. *Journal of the American Medical Association, 288*(10), 1235-1244.

Skhiri, D., Annabi, S., & Allani, D. (1982). Enfants d'immigres: Facteurs de ines ou de rupture? *Annales Medico Psychologiques, 140,* 597-602.

Southern Poverty Law Center. (2003, June). *SPLC report: Immigrants face deadly threats as vigilante violence increases, 33*(2). Retrieved November 29, 2003, from http://www.splcenter.org/center/splcreport/article.jsp?aid=33

Stanton, A. M. (1980). When mothers go to jail. *Criminal Justice* Abstract, 1968-2000/03, San Diego State University. Retrieved June 16, 2000, from wysiwyg://118/http://webspirs.silverplatter.com:8000/calstate

Stein, B. N. (1986). The experience of being a refugee: Insights from the research literature. In C. L. Williams and J. Westermeyer (Eds.), *Refugee mental health in resettlement countries* (pp. 5-23). Washington, DC: Hemisphere.

Sydeman, S. J. (1997). Procedural justice in the context of civil commitment. *Psychology, Public Policy and Law, 207,* 210-211.

Thabat, A. A. (2002). Emotional problems in Palestinian children living in a war zone: A cross-sectional study. *The Lancet, 359*(9320), 1801-1804.

Tucker, J. C., Marx, J., & Long, L. (1998). "Moving on": Residential mobility and children's school lives. *Heritage Foundation, 71,* 111-129.

United States Citizenship and Immigration Services, Office of Immigration Statistics. (2002). *Yearbook of Office of Immigration Statistics.* Retrieved November 12, 2003, from http://uscis.gov/graphics/shared/aboutus/statistics/workload.htm

United States Court of Appeals for the Ninth Circuit. (2003, October 17). Opinion. #01-50376, pp. 15121-15152 (USA v. Isidro Ubaldo-Figueroa). Retrieved December 29, 2003, from http://caselaw.lp.findlaw.com/scripts/getcase.pl?navby=year7court=9th&YEAR2=2003&MONTH=10

Waddell, B. (1999, Fall). Not so permanent: The effect of a criminal conviction on immigrants. *Guild Practitioner,* pp. 190-195.

Ward, C., Bochner, S., & Furnham, A. (2001). *The psychology of culture shock.* London: Routledge.

Willette, R. (2003, Fall). Decades of discrimination. *ColorLines, 6*(3), 13-15.

Williams, D. R., Yu, Y., Jackson, J. S., & Anderson, N. B. (1997). Racial differences in physical and mental health: Socio-economic status, stress and discrimination. *Journal of Health Psychology, 2,* 335-351.

Yaari, A. (1999). Chronic pain in Holocaust survivors. *Journal of Pain and Symptom Management, 17*(3), 181-186.

Yehuda, R. (2003, April). Changes in the concept of PTSD and trauma. *Psychiatric Times,* p. 35.

Zadvydas v. Davis, 121 S. Ct. 2491, 150 L. Ed. 2d 653 (U.S. 2001) remanded to 257 F 3d 1095 (9th Cir. 2001).

# APPENDIX 1

## *Linear Correlations Between Variables*

| | E1 | E2 | E3 | E4 | E5 | E6 | E7 | S1 | S2 | S3 | S4 | S5 | S6 | S7 | S8 | S9 | S12 | S14 | S17 | S19 | S20 | S21 |
|-----|------|------|------|------|------|------|------|------|------|------|------|------|------|------|------|------|------|------|------|------|------|------|
| E1 | 1.00 | | | | | | | | | | | | | | | | | | | | | |
| E2 | 0.19 | 1.00 | | | | | | | | | | | | | | | | | | | | |
| E3 | 0.06 | 0.31 | 1.00 | | | | | | | | | | | | | | | | | | | |
| E4 | 0.27 | 0.24 | 0.08 | 1.00 | | | | | | | | | | | | | | | | | | |
| E5 | 0.13 | -0.01 | -0.14 | 0.08 | 1.00 | | | | | | | | | | | | | | | | | |
| E6 | 0.08 | 0.09 | 0.06 | 0.23 | 0.13 | 1.00 | | | | | | | | | | | | | | | | |
| E7 | 0.03 | 0.21 | 0.10 | 0.25 | 0.28 | 0.30 | 1.00 | | | | | | | | | | | | | | | |
| S1 | 0.15 | 0.11 | -0.01 | -0.01 | 0.13 | 0.46 | 0.22 | 1.00 | | | | | | | | | | | | | | |
| S2 | -0.08 | 0.14 | 0.10 | 0.16 | 0.01 | 0.27 | 0.26 | 0.08 | 1.00 | | | | | | | | | | | | | |
| S3 | 0.08 | 0.29 | 0.03 | 0.33 | 0.12 | 0.31 | 0.34 | 0.19 | 0.07 | 1.00 | | | | | | | | | | | | |
| S4 | 0.11 | 0.01 | -0.07 | 0.21 | 0.17 | 0.13 | 0.04 | 0.07 | 0.04 | 0.15 | 1.00 | | | | | | | | | | | |
| S5 | 0.13 | 0.40 | 0.09 | 0.17 | -0.01 | -0.01 | 0.07 | 0.02 | 0.12 | 0.09 | 0.01 | 1.00 | | | | | | | | | | |
| S6 | 0.07 | -0.02 | 0.06 | 0.06 | 0.06 | 0.31 | 0.05 | 0.30 | 0.18 | 0.10 | 0.01 | -0.06 | 1.00 | | | | | | | | | |
| S7 | 0.05 | 0.00 | 0.13 | -0.02 | 0.16 | 0.08 | 0.21 | -0.05 | 0.01 | 0.22 | -0.07 | 0.05 | -0.02 | 1.00 | | | | | | | | |
| S8 | 0.06 | -0.06 | -0.02 | 0.06 | 0.05 | 0.18 | 0.10 | 0.17 | 0.07 | 0.20 | 0.05 | 0.03 | 0.36 | 0.30 | 1.00 | | | | | | | |
| S9 | -0.07 | 0.02 | -0.02 | -0.02 | -0.09 | 0.03 | 0.02 | -0.01 | 0.24 | -0.09 | -0.03 | 0.02 | 0.30 | -0.05 | 0.05 | 1.00 | | | | | | |
| S12 | 0.05 | 0.22 | 0.01 | 0.13 | -0.01 | 0.07 | 0.20 | 0.07 | -0.05 | 0.54 | 0.12 | 0.01 | -0.03 | 0.12 | 0.06 | -0.05 | 1.00 | | | | | |
| S14 | 0.05 | 0.00 | -0.04 | -0.09 | 0.01 | 0.14 | 0.12 | 0.34 | -0.07 | 0.06 | -0.04 | 0.00 | 0.04 | 0.22 | 0.29 | -0.02 | 0.11 | 1.00 | | | | |
| S17 | -0.06 | 0.00 | -0.08 | 0.18 | -0.06 | 0.07 | 0.04 | -0.09 | -0.07 | -0.02 | -0.04 | 0.12 | -0.03 | 0.13 | 0.03 | -0.02 | -0.06 | 0.23 | 1.00 | | | |
| S19 | -0.04 | -0.06 | 0.02 | 0.13 | 0.06 | -0.07 | -0.06 | -0.06 | -0.05 | 0.04 | -0.02 | -0.04 | -0.02 | -0.04 | 0.04 | -0.02 | 0.04 | -0.02 | -0.02 | 1.00 | | |
| S20 | -0.03 | -0.08 | -0.07 | -0.02 | -0.04 | 0.07 | 0.02 | 0.06 | -0.06 | -0.04 | -0.03 | 0.02 | -0.03 | -0.05 | -0.05 | -0.02 | -0.05 | -0.02 | 0.27 | -0.02 | 1.00 | |
| S21 | -0.01 | -0.04 | -0.07 | 0.00 | 0.07 | 0.06 | 0.21 | -0.04 | 0.06 | 0.14 | -0.06 | 0.03 | 0.29 | 0.56 | 0.42 | -0.04 | 0.01 | 0.27 | 0.27 | 0.06 | -0.04 | 1.00 |
| S25 | 0.08 | 0.09 | 0.02 | -0.06 | -0.07 | -0.07 | 0.09 | 0.16 | -0.05 | 0.08 | -0.02 | 0.07 | -0.02 | -0.04 | -0.04 | -0.02 | 0.27 | 0.44 | 0.21 | -0.01 | -0.02 | -0.03 |

# APPENDIX B

## *Issue Paper: The 1996 Immigration Laws Are Unjust*

BRENNAN CENTER FOR JUSTICE
AT NYU SCHOOL OF LAW
Public Policy Advocacy Clinic
Prof. Nancy Morawetz, Co-Director

A decorated US veteran who fought in the Gulf War is being deported because of a single conviction for which he received a sentence of one year. He has been a legal permanent resident of the US for 25 years, since he was 11 years old. He is married to a US citizen and is the father of two US citizen children. Every day they live in fear that their father will be taken away from them.

A single mother of a US citizen child is being deported because of a 1980 conviction for which she received a probationary sentence and no jail time. She moved to the United States in 1960 and has been a legal permanent resident since she was three years old. Her entire family resides in the US and she is the primary care provider for both her minor child and her elderly mother.

A US citizen mother of four fears that she will be forced onto public assistance because her legal permanent resident husband was recently put in detention after serving his criminal sentence. She fears that her husband will be deported to Italy and forever separated from her and their US citizen children.

### THE PROBLEM

Harsh new immigration laws regarding the deportation of legal residents with criminal convictions are turning the lives of many US citizens and legal permanent residents upside down and ruthlessly tearing families apart. The Illegal Immigration Reform and Immigrant Responsibility Act (IIRAIRA) and the Anti-Terrorism and Effective Death Penalty Act (AEDPA) deny legal residents fundamental due process rights and are being retroactively applied to legal residents with criminal convictions.

These laws make many legal immigrants deportable for relatively minor crimes and leave the vast majority ineligible for relief from deportation by prohibiting immigration judges from hearing people's individual circumstances.

## WHY THE LAWS NEED TO BE CHANGED

Retroactive application of these laws flies in the face of our system of law and traditional notions of justice. Applying the law retroactively adds new burdens to already settled matters, undermining our system of justice. Moreover, people made decisions about their criminal cases, for example, whether to accept or reject pleas, based on the law as it existed at that time. The retroactive application of these laws changes the rules in the middle of the game, a concept universally recognized as unfair.

Many legal residents are unfairly denied the opportunity to apply for relief from deportation. Many can no longer appear before an immigration judge who could consider individual circumstances, such as rehabilitation since the crime, family ties to the US, length of residency in the US, how long ago the crime was committed, severity of the crime, lack of ties to and/or inability to speak the language of [the] country of origin, and other compelling factors. Under the new laws, such factors are completely ignored.

The 1996 laws expanded the definition of "aggravated felony" to include a broad range of relatively minor crimes, many of which are nonviolent and are misdemeanors under state laws.

The expanded definition has many new implications which were not contemplated when the term was first introduced. The term "aggravated felony" serves not only to define who is deportable, but also who is subject to many other penalties under the law, such as dentention, ineligibility [for] relief from deportation, and permanent inadmissibility to the United States.

Many legal residents are unfairly subject to mandatory detention. People who have already served their criminal sentences (or even those who served no time) are taken away from their families and are placed into an INS detention center or prison. Moreover, those in detention are denied a bond hearing in which they may be able to show that they pose no threat to society, are not a flight risk, have already served their criminal sentence, have rehabilitated, are productively living in their communities and/or financially supporting their families. Detaining non-violent legal residents, many of whom are the primary income providers for their US citizen and legal permanent resident families, leaves families financially and emotionally destitute.

Federal courts have been stripped of judicial review, insulating the INS from mistakes, oversights and abuse of discretion.  Judicial review is a fundamental component of our justice system, a system built on checks and balances.  Giving the INS, a government agency, such absolute power leaves no way to monitor if the laws are being enforced correctly and justly.  An administrative agency is left completely unaccountable for its decisions.


## SOLUTIONS

Fairness must be reintroduced to the deportation process.  Congress must enact legislation to remedy the gross injustices produced by the 1996 laws.

This legislation should:
-- Eliminate retroactive application of the laws
-- Restore discretion to immigration judges to consider individual circumstances: change the eligibility requirements for cancellation of removal
-- Modify the definition of "aggravated felony" to encompass only serious crimes
-- Change the mandatory detention rules and institute bond hearings
-- Reinstate judicial review

# APPENDIX C

*Global Consequences of IIRAIRA*

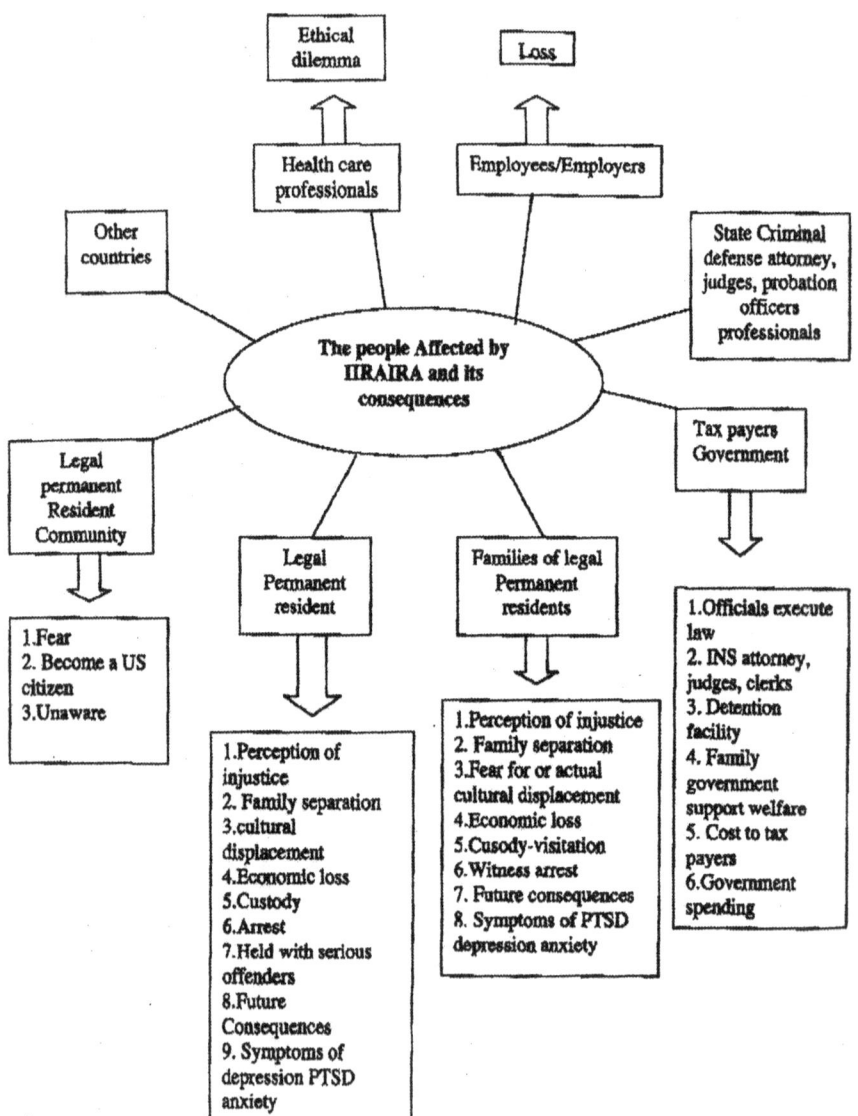

978-0-595-37333-8
0-595-37333-X

www.ingramcontent.com/pod-product-compliance
Lightning Source LLC
Chambersburg PA
CBHW051438280526
45785CB00003B/1338